a BEAUTIFUL
kind of
BROKEN

a BEAUTIFUL
kind of
BROKEN

THE POWER OF IDENTITY

LUKE
HOLTER

Dedication

This book is dedicated to

my lovely wife,

Grace.

You are God's gift to me...

the reason I wake up every morning.

Special Dedication

To Papa Bear and Momma Bird...

I would like to thank my mother and father for their unrelenting faith, dedication, love, and compassion. They have been unwavering in their steadfastness with the Lord. My parents never gave up on me even when they had plenty of reason to do just that. They have paid my rent and my bills (medical and living expenses), and have poured themselves out in my life in more ways than I could ever possibly recount.

I have seen my mother and father give of themselves for over 30 years to the church and the broken. They are true heroes of the faith. I have seen them give their all to their family and friends over the course of my childhood and up through my adult years. They have had their hearts broken by family, friends, and God. But they have come through as pure gold, as strong authentic Christians.

They have loved me through piercings, a rainbow of hairstyles and colors, many, many, many tattoos (ha-ha, sorry,

Mom), and they have loved me through much suffering, heartache, and disappointment. My mother and father have given till it hurts and have continuously offered love as from a deep well.

Barry and Cheri Holter…this is for you. Thank you for never failing each other, your faith, or your family. You believed in me when I couldn't believe in myself. This book is for you. I love you both.

Acknowledgments

I'd like to give special thanks to…

God, Jesus, Holy Spirit (my best friends), my wife, Grace, Barry and Cheri Holter, Mark and Jeannie Holter, Joy and Mike Myers, Rubin and Catherine Laurel, The Laurel Family, Grandma & Grandpa Laurel, Darin Crawford (the only class in this act), Calvin Campbell, Rachel Hargrave, Rich Albrecht, The Abuegs, Jason and Jodi Morse, Jake Stuessy, Jake Abueg, Kathy Hahn, J. Kevin and Sandra Munz with Cullen's Upscale American Grille, The Elijah List, Steve Shultz, Lou Engle, Mike Bickle, Paul Cain, Bill Johnson, Patricia King, Shawn Bolz, Bobby Conner, Rob Hotchkin, LaVonne Chandler, Jon Brown, Chuck and Trista Smith, Tim and Sue Myers, Craig and Stephanie Schumaier, Peggy and Larry Schumaier, Bonnie Berryman, Larry Stenson, and The Fire Starters.

Endorsements

Psalm 51:17 declares, "The sacrifices of God are a broken spirit: a broken and contrite heart, O God thou wilt not despise." (KJV) Luke Holter's new book builds and releases the reader into this undiscovered country so few are willing to venture into. Luke has not only begun to emerge as a prophetic messenger, but as one who will help a generation of believers walk in their call and destiny.

Paul Cain
Paulcain.org

Luke Holter's book, *A Beautiful Kind of Broken,* is an excellent read. I loved the title when the manuscript was sent to me. It intrigued me. I could hardly wait to find out what it actually meant. "What is it?" I asked myself. "What could possibly be so beautiful about being broken?"

Now, I understand. Why don't you find out too! If you do, you will be enriched and empowered.

Patricia King
Xpmedia.com

Luke Holter is quickly becoming a clear voice for this generation. Luke's unique perspective is like a bright shining light illuminating with clarity. I love watching friends of God emerge and take their place in the Kingdom, and that is exactly what God is doing with my new friend, Luke. He has been hearing the Lord very clearly in this season and has had understanding to help people position their hearts and faith.

Shawn Bolz, Senior Pastor
Expression58 Ministries

Contents

Foreword

I think we now live in a mature enough age where people realize that God uses broken vessels to display His glory. He went after Peter, a common fisherman who was probably in his early twenties and not very educated in the law. He went after the tax collector, the prostitute, and the Samaritan woman. He pursued people in the Bible who were not healthy when He pursued them, but He could see them in their fullness as if they were everything the Father dreamed of them being. He treated each of them with the full invitation as a healthy wonderful person now, not at the end of their journey when they proved it, and because of that He had friends who became His dream. They fulfilled the hopes and dreams He had in his heart

Why was Peter so zealously loyal in his friendship with Jesus that he fought guards to protect Him the night that Jesus was being betrayed by Judas? Because Jesus had changed Peter's perception of God. He had become friends with Peter, and they had intimacy and a love bond that was enough to cause Peter to put himself at risk to protect the very object of his love. Jesus made God accessible to everyone and targeted a crowd that was the opposite of what anyone would have thought He would run after when He came.

Not only that, but Jesus dealt with people who doubted God's nature—like Thomas. He had friends who would interrupt the common, normal protocol, and wash His feet with perfume—like Mary. He had friends who would hang out up in trees out of desperation to meet Him—like Zacchaeus. Even established society members and people who had a lot to lose (their reputations) came to Him and performed radical acts out of their brokenness to get just a moment with Jesus. Why? Because they saw Someone who was not only safe, but also Someone who could heal their core and give them what they were so hungry for. Jesus saw beauty in the broken people.

You and I are in a generation where we can obviously see that the world is broken; we can see what doesn't work or is unhealthy. What if God is actually attracted to broken people and what if He can make brokenness beautiful? What if the tools of the Kingdom that heal people are as simple as having a relationship of intimacy with God and the truth of His Word? The Bible was written for all people from all walks of life—from the uneducated pygmies in Africa to kings and rulers—and it provides an on-ramp for the highway of holiness. Holiness is the quality or state of being holy, set apart, not profane, not undone in wrong ways but completely shining, being fully able to share in God's nature.

This was Jesus' great desire for us when He went to the cross, that He could take our shame, our curses, our pain, and our brokenness, and in return give us back a restoration to that place of intimate fellowship with God. He surrendered all so that we could enter into completeness, even in the midst of surrendering ourselves throughout our life to this beautiful process of overcoming.

Luke's book is for people who are awesome but who have areas of life that they haven't yet overcome. In fact, it is an overcomers' manual full of practical wisdom. It is also a guide that church and ministry leaders can use to assist them in creating healthy community.

Rejection, anxiety, and fear are complicated issues. It is difficult to make the truth accessible in the midst of them, but that is what Luke has been able to do in this book.

What I love about this book is that you get the opportunity to go on Luke's journey. A person's life story is like a picture, and just like the old saying goes, "A picture is worth a thousand words." Luke's life story is worth a thousand sermons that you could get on these subjects that he has filled the book with.

So read on. Grab hold of simple truth in the context of your relationship to the heart of God. Go on the journey that this book provides, and surely you will feel yourself far more connected to the heart of God than ever before.

Shawn Bolz
Senior Pastor of Expression58
Author of *Keys to Heaven's Economy* and
Throne Room Company

Preface

The purpose of this book is to equip people with the tools for overcoming rejection and spiritual abuse using my own story, biblical fact, the love of Jesus, and the revelatory power of the Holy Spirit.

I am not interested in providing easy answers for everyone who is hurting. The truth is that I don't think there are easy answers.

You were created to be unique, and so your journey out of pain and rejection will have a certain amount of uniqueness as well. I will provide you with my story and what I find to be the Spirit of Truth on these issues. But in order for you to go along on this journey, you must put your motives and personal character into the hands of God. You must trust God with your pain and your insecurities. Only He can set you up for a divine encounter on the road of truth.

Let me assure you that the information I share in this book is based on my own personal experience and education as well as the actual experiences of real people whose accounts can be independently verified and who, to the best of my knowledge, have been truthful about their encounters with community, rejection, and spiritual abuse. There is a blaring siren sounding in the Church telling us that a serious problem exists in our Church communities. I did not use anyone's real name in this book, and I do not share any personal stories of their journeys. What qualifies me as an author to write on this subject is my education on exit counseling (cult counseling) as well as my own experience dealing with leaders who have themselves crossed the line of healthy relationship with me. I earned my Bachelor's degree from North Carolina College of Theology and have extensive education in Christian counseling and cognitive therapy. I am also a member of the American Association of Christian Counselors. It is my hope that this book will provide the catalyst and the context for healing, forgiveness, and understanding—both in you as an individual, and in the community of believers.

Know that as you start this progressive journey, you will deal with anger, sadness, love, forgiveness, blame, shame, and an assortment of other feelings that will come to the surface through this process. Be of great courage, because if you say *yes* to this journey, the Lord will heal your mind and rebuild your heart!

Introduction

MY HISTORY WITH REJECTION

I am the son of a preacher man. Yes, I grew up with the wonderful childhood experience of being a pastor's kid—and that, in and of itself, could be the basis for a book on rejection and spiritual abuse (insert sarcasm here). Growing up in church was a beautifully broken experience. I had the curse and privilege of being related to about 70 percent of my church family, and *that*, my friend, can make for a difficult and dysfunctional situation in the process of growing and developing through childhood.

It's hard for pastors' kids to grow up and not become jaded with the whole process of church and ministry. I have a great deal of respect and compassion for the children of ministry leaders. I myself became a prodigal for seven years due to my own issues of rejection and my misinterpretation of that rejection in God's view of me.

Let me say this to the hurting children of ministry: God loves you very much, and you did not let Him down. (I feel the Holy Spirit on me even now as I am writing to ALL who are broken and hurting.) You all must know that God is very pleased with you and that you have never frustrated His patience nor caused Him to be disgusted with you. You need to know that nothing you have done could ever, *ever* separate you from the love of Jesus.

I was diagnosed with ADD (Attention Deficit Disorder) in the third grade. I was put on medication that I took in secret and was put in "special" classes throughout my school career. I felt rejected at church, school, home, work, and in relationships, plus I often dealt with self-rejection as well.

The truth is that we all deal with some level of rejection and abuse. Those who are in the church or who grew up in the church seem to be special targets for this type of thing. The real questions are: *What do we do with the pain?* and *Where do we take our wounds?*

As I grew up, I learned new and innovative ways to be rejected. When I was a child, few people knew very much about ADD or how to relate to children who have this disorder. I was tested and medicated to help me deal with my "problem" of inattention. I remember when I was put in a special education classroom an hour a day to get help with my homework. I would hide so no one could find me. I had to be sneaky when I did attend these "special classes" so none of my peers would see me go into this class.

The special education classroom was generally for children who were severely mentally and physically handicapped. I was surrounded by many varieties of intense disabilities in this classroom. So, I guess, internal rejection as well as social rejection became commonplace in my life at an early age. I used to hide in the basement hallways at school until the bell rang for class, so no one would see me enter the special needs classroom. I used to sit at a round table working on schoolwork with special needs kids screaming and having seizures all around me. My classmates would walk by the open door and see me sitting there with these special needs children, and later they would make fun of me for being in that classroom.

I grew up with an estranged extended family. I was close and in love with my immediate family, but I was not close with my aunts, uncles, and most of my cousins. This history in part is what inspired me to become a Christian counselor. I desired to understand rejection and interpersonal relationships. I have a history of participation in movements and church communities where I have had to face the spirit of rejection. In my 20+ years as a Christian living in a church community, I have watched my family and loved ones walk through the fire of rejection and spiritual abuse. I have been told that I needed to marry someone, and I have had leaders forbid me to be friends with others outside the "fold." I have seen and been a part of terrible acts of elitism in leadership, and I have begged for acceptance when the tables were turned on me.

That is just a brief overview of my history and experience with rejection, pain, and abuse. In the following chapters, I will share more of my life story along with what I've learned along the way.

REJECTION

My story is not entirely unique. Many people have grown up with similar issues and problems. As unique as we all are in gender, race, upbringing, and belief system, we have one thing that commonly stitches together the fabric of our culture. The one thing that we all have to face at some point in our lives is the Spirit of Rejection.

Rejection can be a tool used by God to mature us and grow us, and it can also be used by satan to harm us and keep us from growing. This leaves us with an interesting question: How do we respond when rejection comes? What do we do with our pain, low self-esteem, and feelings of inadequacy? When rejection comes, who do we take it to?

This is such a provoking thought for me. On a larger scale, we tend to blame God when we think He has wounded us, and we tend to grab hold of the accusations from the enemy and make them our own thoughts and identity. We get trapped into viewing God, the enemy, and ourselves through the wrong filters. We reject God and take on the identity of the very one who seeks to destroy our hearts.

Oftentimes we get tempted and spend our energy repenting to God for "thinking those thoughts." The truth needs to be made clear in our minds and hearts through the power of the Holy Spirit and revelation from the Word of God. We struggle with temptation in part because we don't have a proper working biblical understanding, and our hearts have not been awakened by the Holy Spirit. We should, as a people, celebrate when the Holy Spirit has given us the strength to say *no* to temptation, but instead we often find ourselves apologizing for thinking impure thoughts. Did you know that if temptation comes and you don't cross a line into fantasy about that temptation, then YOU WIN, and the Lord is proud of you for being able to stand!

When we give in to the temptation, we give it life and power. We allow temptation to cross the line into sin when we fantasize about the temptation. Instead, we must get into the place of knowing who we are and who God really is. We must become educated on the nature and character of God. And we must be doers of the Word of God (see James 1:22). We must fill up our hearts with intimacy unto revelation so we can give the Holy Spirit something to work with!

A lot of pain can come from rejection, and that makes it tricky when processing the pain and wounding that can be associated with being rejected. In some way, all of us have tried to erect walls that will protect us from rejection. We are haunted by our own history of rejection, and we try our best to resolve these old ghosts in various ways.

I conducted a series of social experiments where I asked one question of several friends and acquaintances, including people of different genders, race, and faiths. I asked them, "Are you affected by rejection?" And the overwhelming response was, "I don't really allow other people's opinions to affect me." Some people would make the statement, "Others can't hurt me." At times you could see people shrink back with teary eyes, still proclaiming that they are unaffected when others reject or hurt them.

The truth is that we are deeply wounded when rejected by others. We as people desire affirmation from others, and when we don't get it—no matter how confident we like to think we are—we still tend to feel rejected. Even saying, "I am unaffected by rejection," can be a way to protect oneself. The fact that we must have any kind of protective mechanism to buffer us from rejection shows us that perhaps it has pierced our hearts on a deeper level than we would care or feel comfortable to admit?

What tends to also happen within this same vicious cycle of rejection is something called "bitter root judgment." This is when you have been hurt by rejection and you say to yourself, "I will never allow that to happen to me again," or when rejected by a parent, you say, "I will never be like my mother or father." However, the problem with bitter root judgment is that you become what you despise because it's all you are focusing on. As a society, we tend to worship what we fear. We become what we behold. It is the *beholding and becoming* principle in a most broken way.

We were meant to behold God and be transformed into the likeness of His Son, Jesus (see 2 Cor. 3:18). We were created to be in fear of God, which actually means to be in *awe* or *wonder* of God (see Deut. 6:2). What God intended is for us to become like Him, but in the realm of broken human hearts, satan has an opportunity to use that same principle to lie to us and cause us to fear something other than God. That is idolatry. The goal of the enemy at every aspect and at every turn is to steal the worship and adoration of God, from God.

I have had to deal with this issue of rejection on so many levels in my own life. I am not writing this book as a way to say that I have a perfect understanding of rejection or that I have only played the victim. I myself have offended, rejected, and hurt people my whole life. Whether or not I even knew it, others have been rejected by me.

I see the value in diving headfirst into our pain to find a sort of resolution with these issues. I am hoping that along the way you will see the *Jesus* in this book, and my prayer is that the *Jesus* in this book makes His way into your heart through the process.

Now, I do not want to have you on a witch-hunt to constantly be looking for rejection or spiritually abusive situations. My heart is that you would understand walking in forgiveness, and that most of the time rejection is not something done on purpose. This is such a wide topic to even discuss that obviously this book unto itself is not meant for every single circumstance you have been in where you may have felt rejected or abused spiritually. This book is to help us *take our pain and wounds to the cross* and not necessarily to other people.

How we process our wounds and what we do with our pain is one of the most important aspects of rejection, spiritual abuse, and forgiveness. As we go further along in this book, we will discuss the important role that forgiveness plays when addressing rejection and spiritual abuse. Frankly, it *all* hinges on forgiveness. This journey is about forgiving God, others, and yourself.

Rejection Sensitivity

Early psychological theories often referred to the phenomenon of "rejection sensitivity." These theories suggest that because of the broken past of many people who have been hurt in ministries or church, it is more likely that they will develop a form of sensitivity to rejection, or a tendency toward becoming offended on a more frequent basis.

I think that sometimes this "rejection sensitivity" syndrome is more in line with the spirit of rejection. In some cases people can feel offended and rejected because they have a spirit of offense or a gravitation toward being easily rejected. Sometimes we in the Church deal very differently with these issues than the secular world does. I believe it is vital that we approach these issues differently, but I think it will also do the Church a great deal of good to look at the benefits that come from the world of counseling and psychology.

The spirit of rejection is emotionally painful because human beings are social creatures by nature and desire the approval and acceptance of a group or social network. People need both stable relationships and satisfying interactions with the people in those relationships. There are several emotional effects that come from being rejected. The intensity of these effects can vary depending upon several factors. You are likely going to feel these effects regardless of where or who the rejection originates from. However, the intensity of these feelings largely depends upon the depth of relationship you have with the source of the rejection.

Processing Rejection: Four Major Emotions

In his book *Christian Counseling: A Comprehensive Guide*, Dr. Gary R. Collins states that most human beings will go through four major emotions when processing rejection: anxiety, loneliness, depression, and anger.[1] And while I admit that this process may not be the same in everyone, my history, education, and experience as a Christian counselor have shown that it is true for most people.

One of the interesting side effects of feeling rejection or allowing rejection to wound us is that we sometimes portray attributes that cause others to reject us. We feel hurt and wounded from an initial rejection, and thus we exude a personality that causes most other people to reject us. This is a vicious cycle and is evident in the lives of those who have not allowed the Holy Spirit to come in and heal them at the deepest levels of their souls.

In the next section, I will give more information from Dr. Collins's book, *Christian Counseling,* and the four major emotions that most people experience when processing rejection. Due to the broadness of the topic and the space constraints of this book, I will not exhaustively dive into every aspect and emotion. However, I hope to give you the tools to acknowledge these emotions so you can get started on your journey of healing. One of my goals in this book is to help you be able to not just acknowledge what you are feeling, but also choose to move forward into the place of total forgiveness.

Anxiety

The first emotion that individuals usually feel when faced with rejection is anxiety. That shouldn't be too much of a surprise when you consider that it is almost always an unsettling encounter when you find yourself facing rejection. You get that feeling in your gut when you think it's coming, and you brace yourself for the blow. I know that in my own history when I felt like rejection was rearing its ugly head my way, my mind would race. I would think all sorts of unhealthy thoughts on behalf of the individual or institution that was getting ready to lower the earth-quaking boom of rejection. We can find ourselves in a very unhealthy state of mind when we become anxious concerning the possibility of rejection.

Anxiety is one of the most common emotions of our time. We all feel it and it permeates our culture through television, Internet, radio, movies, etc. We seem to be a culture that can't just settle down and relax. We find ourselves to be a people controlled by fear.

Anxiety can best be summed up as an inner feeling of apprehension or worry. It is the feeling of dread you experience when facing a situation that you feel could end ultimately with your expulsion or rejection from an individual or group. What is actually taking place in your body is something called "fight or flight." This is the body's response to a perceived threat or danger. During this reaction, certain hormones like adrenalin and cortisol are released, speeding the heart rate, slowing digestion, shunting blood flow to major muscle groups, and changing various other autonomic nervous functions, giving the body a burst of energy and strength. Originally named for its ability to enable us to physically fight or run away when faced with danger, it's now activated in situations where neither response is appropriate, like in traffic or during a stressful day at work.

On a physical level, this involves an increase in heart rate and blood pressure, as well as neurological changes. It is not uncommon for people suffering from anxiety to feel faint, dizzy, or aggressive.

A side note on anxiety: it is not always caused by a legitimately threatening situation. Oftentimes you can feel anxiety from an imaginary threat or simply from the uncertainty of "what *could* happen."

I find that the best way to help prevent anxiety is to go to the Word of God and rely upon the power of the Holy Spirit to work within you a calming and peaceful state of mind (see Phil. 4:6). When we pray, things happen. As we walk out godly behavior through the revelation of the Word and the empowerment of the Holy Spirit, we mature; and as we submit our minds to the truth of Scripture, we can process anxiety in a healthy and biblical manner.

Trusting God doesn't mean that we don't admit what we are feeling or pretend like the feelings aren't there. What it means is that we trust God with what we feel. God gave us emotion, and for too long the Church has conducted itself in a manner that implies it is unsafe to be human or to show emotion. God desperately desires us to live out of the fullness of our God-given emotions.

Loneliness

Loneliness is a topic that I could easily write an entire book on. In my opinion, it is the hardest form of human suffering that a person can bear. Ever since the fall of humankind, there is a gamut of emotions that we must process—none of which I believe to be more debilitating than loneliness Jesus understood what it meant to be lonely here on earth. Often times Jesus went off to be alone in prayer. Jesus understood the human condition of loneliness and that's why He gave us a promise in the book of Hebrews promising that He would never leave us or forsake us (see Heb. 13:5).

In *Christian Counseling*, Dr. Collins tells us that sociologist Robert Weiss estimated that a quarter of the American population feels extremely lonely at some time during any given month. Loneliness affects people of every age, class, sex, and race. The most commonly affected groups are those governments or people groups that make individualism the main focal point of their society or community structure.

The causes of loneliness are many, but they can be grouped into five categories: social, developmental, psychological, situational, and spiritual.

Loneliness often increases during times of change and distress. This may account for higher reports of loneliness among young people in post-high school years. It can also be due to rapid social changes in our sphere of history. Some of the social changes that can escalate the feeling of loneliness are technology, mobility, urbanization, and television. Part of the reason that loneliness comes when processing rejection is due to the very nature of isolation that can be associated with rejection. Often times when we feel we have been rejected, we become isolated in our wound thus providing the perfect formula for loneliness and even more isolation and rejection from that loneliness. When we can be kept isolated through our own thoughts, we further the damage of rejection and loneliness.

Depression

Depression is a side effect of rejection simply because it can often be brought about through isolation and loneliness. Depression is a worldwide phenomenon that affects individuals of all ages, and it appears to be increasing among teenagers and young adults. According to *Christian Counseling*, depression disrupts the lives of an estimated 30 to 40 million people in the United States alone.

It is worth noting that a large percentage of the staff and population of better-known ministries are young adults. Thus the increasing incidence of depression in this age group needs to be considered when a ministry leader is trying to encourage the emotional well-being of his or her staff. We must ensure that we are providing an emotionally healthy environment for those in any church or ministry community.

Anger

Oftentimes Christians feel that emotions are evil, when in fact, God created them. Anger, for example, is often misconstrued as a bad thing when, in reality, not all angry emotions are a "bad thing." It is often very healthy to be angry when you are hurt and walking through forgiveness, or when you are protecting yourself or a loved one. The Bible says, *"Do not sin in your anger"* (Eph. 4:26), which leaves it open to the reader to infer that anger itself is not sinful or demonic. However, in our immaturity, anger can become something wielded by the demonic.

In addition, a lot of people have hidden anger. I personally believe that anger that is hidden and not exposed or admitted before the Father is the kind of anger that can take on an unhealthy life. When we suppress our emotions, they often boil over into sin. You see, we were created to live out of the openness and fullness of our unique personalities and the fullness of our emotions before God.

Hidden anger that is acted out either subconsciously or deliberately is typically called *passive aggression*. There are many ways that you can unknowingly walk out passive aggression toward yourself or others around you. It can manifest itself in ways you would never imagine. For example, you can subconsciously punish others by being forgetful. In some cases of passive aggression, the individual who is angry with themselves will even subconsciously become very accident prone or "clumsy," leading to self-injury. The good news is that by addressing these issues before the Lord, often with the help of a counselor and prayer, you can shed light on these situations, thus leading to a break in the cycle of passive aggression.

Passive aggression is a self-made prison for the individual feeling the anger and the one that the passive aggression is aimed at. Maybe not imprisons them both in the same way but maybe the word affects them both. When we become passively aggressive, we step into what I feel is a unique kind of manipulation. Through passive anger, we can begin to give unfair criticism and character assassination to others around us. At times, others can even have well-meaning intentions that trigger an eruption (they are related) of anger within us toward that individual or someone else that we are holding spiritually hostage. If we will open ourselves to the work of the Holy Spirit, He will show us the areas in our life where we might be conducting ourselves in a hidden destructive manner.

In *Christian Counseling*, Dr. Collins states that anger, openly displayed, deliberately hidden from others, or unconsciously expressed, is the root of many psychological, interpersonal, physical, and spiritual problems. Along with hostility, anger has been called "the chief saboteur of the mind," and "the leading cause of misery, depression, inefficiency, sickness, accidents, loss of work time and financial loss in industry."[2] No matter what the problem—marital conflict, alcoholism, a wife's frigidity, a child's defiance, and nervous or physical disease—elimination of hostility is a key factor in its solution.

Like anxiety, anger is aroused through the "fight or flight" area of human makeup. As I mentioned earlier, when this feeling of fight or flight arises, it is not always due to a physical threat. Oftentimes, when you are wounded emotionally, you can react in a way that ensures protection. Rejection can very easily come across as a threat. Although it may not be a physical threat, the fear of rejection is a very real thing. When your body senses a threat, it releases chemical reactions that can lead to increased heart rate, increased perspiration, pupil dilation, and other biological changes that get you ready to either run or fight.

When looking at anger, or any other emotion, you must try to do what you can to stay balanced in your perspective. Truth and perception are not always the same thing. There could be something that someone has done that has made you very angry, but you may have seriously misread the situation or the individual.

In these modern times, it has become easy to unleash our misguided anger through technology. I cannot tell you how many emails I have written or others have written to me that have been totally misread and misinterpreted. Through the Internet, email, and online forums or web communities, we have been given an alternate reality when it comes to human interaction. In many ways, technology has furthered us as a people, but in other ways, it has caused us to become more distant and isolated.

What would happen if we were all brave and we spoke the truth in love to the best of our human ability? What kind of beautiful things might happen if we just admitted that we were hurt and angry?

We could make leaps and bounds as a Church and as believers if we walked in the openness that we were called to live in. We could radically remake the current church system if we embraced our emotions and lived out of the Kingdom of Love.

The Battle Within

All of the emotional conditions that we have discussed in this chapter will be unique to each individual. To some degree there are things that will be the same across the board, but just as we each were created with uniqueness, we will also experience our emotions with uniqueness. No two people experience this common condition in the same way.

We so often find ourselves in a battle—the battle within. We find ourselves at war with ourselves more often than we may realize, and the mind is the very field on which this war is fought. The mind and the manner by which we process things are vital to our ability to allow the Holy Spirit to use what God created (our mind, will, and emotions) to overcome the destructive moods caused by our thought patterns.

In order to rise above any mood that is not healthy or conducive to our overall well-being, we must change our thought life. Allowing the Holy Spirit to help us change the way we think is crucial. We have to allow our old patterns of thought to be challenged by the Holy Spirit.

Almost all behavior and mood are tied to thought. In most instances, this is a proven reality and fact. We can greatly improve our overall mood, physical health, and general outlook on life simply by allowing the Holy Spirit to come in and renew our mind. The mind is tied to the heart. What we think about, we will follow, and that applies to both moods and actions (see Phil. 2:5 and Rom. 12:2).

Therefore, we must challenge our thinking process. We all have a subconscious tape loop that plays an internal audible identity code within us. This self-talk plays over and over again through our minds, often convincing us of either positive or harmful things about our identity.

To challenge this thinking process, you must first be aware that it is going on. Take stock of what you are feeling. Ask yourself, "Why do I feel sad or depressed?" Then, trace through your thought patterns for the day that may possibly have led up to this mood or behavior. To challenge that reality is to challenge the internal self-talk.

Let's say, for instance, that you say to yourself, "I am stupid" or "I am incompetent." What is the true evidence for the view that you are stupid? In what areas do you feel that you are incompetent? Is it OK to not know everything, or to be incompetent in some areas?

When we are able to trace our thought life and patterns and thus challenge the destructive patterns, then we are able to greatly diminish the severity of our moods and behaviors. We will see a noticeable measure of breakthrough in our depression or harmful moods and behaviors. When we are empowered by the Holy Spirit to change (meaning the Holy Spirit gives us the strength to keep renewing our minds), then we will be able to pour that same strength into the inaccurate identities of those around us as well.

Questions

1. When someone opens up to you and allows herself to be vulnerable, how do you relate to her after that?

2. Do you find yourself belittling him or being over-sensitive to his walk after that point?

3. Where are you taking *your* pain?

Endnotes

1. Dr. Gary R. Collins, *Christian Counseling: A Comprehensive Guide* (Nashville, TN: Thomas Nelson, 2007).

2. Milton Layden, *Escaping the Hostility Trap* (Englewood Cliffs, NJ: Prentice, 1977).

IDENTITY THROUGH ACCEPTANCE

The fact that we are rejected in life means that we, in some way, shape, or form, have to process that rejection mentally, relationally, and emotionally. Now, some people say that to overcome rejection, you must come to a place of self-dependence or self-reliance. Some authors who have written on this subject say that you do not need acceptance from people. They say that we need to come to a place where we are literally unaffected by the admiration or rejection of others.

In basic theory, I understand where these people are coming from, and I agree that we should be able to stand firm on who we are in Christ. I understand the concept of getting our identity from the Lord. But I also think that being overly zealous for independence can be isolating and can rob us of our God-given humanity. Humanity was created to depend on one another. It is a God design.

Mike Bickle, the director of the International House of Prayer Missions Base of Kansas City (IHOP–KC), offers some really great perspectives on identity. I was inspired to begin my own journey toward finding identity while sitting under Mike's teachings during my time as a leader at IHOP-KC. One valuable truth I learned while I was serving at IHOP-KC was the fact that we all need other people. Yes, I admitted that we all need people.

We need to be the hands, words, and actions of Jesus to this world as well as to our fellow believers within the Church. We were called to speak into one another's lives through encouragement, love, affirmation, and hospitality. We need one another to both correct and uplift each other. This is a very basic biblical principle that can be found throughout the Word of God.

Human beings are social creatures by nature, and God designed us that way. At the time of creation, God said that it was not good for man to be alone (see Gen. 2:18). He gave Adam a companion, instructed the human race to multiply (see Gen. 9:7), and has permitted us to expand into the billions of people who now occupy planet Earth.

The over-zealous desire to be self-sufficient can be very damaging in the Church and in ministry communities. We worry so much in some church circles about keeping certain social boundaries that we wind up using these same boundaries as an excuse to *not* love others around us, or to prevent them from being able to love us. Many people take pride in their individualism, self-determination, and independence, but sometimes these traits cut us off from other people and make us more insensitive, lonely, and unable to get along with others. This is not what God intended. Healthy social boundaries should enable us to love others with more wisdom and strength. Healthy boundaries should never push us away from others or drive us to become isolated.

We need to learn to be wise in how we deal with rejection because of the negative situations internally and externally it can cause in a community. Many negative situations can occur as side effects to rejection in a community, and strife is a major one, due in part to the chain reaction that comes from strife. When strife enters the picture because of the hurt or wound of personal rejection, it breeds dissension in the community.

In order for us to have peace in community we must first have peace with God. This is the healthy part of the idea that we should get our identity from God. You see, we need to be confident in who we are in Jesus so that we can—with great strength—love others around us. It's hard to love others when we are so susceptible to being rejected by them. That is why you must first go on this journey of finding out who you are in Christ and who Christ is to you. Once we are in a place of healthy identity, then we can reach out to those around us and get involved in deeper ways in their lives.

As you read this book, you will probably notice that I have one major message: The most important thing is your relationship with the Father and how we are in relationship with Him. This is what possesses my thoughts and soul. I am consumed with this idea that we can do all things that God has called us to do by living out of the reality of our relationship with Him. We can do nothing without Him. We need God to enable us to love God. We need God to enable us to worship God. This is good news.

As we become students of God's emotions, we will grow in revelation of His tender mercy, His gladness, and His affection. Then, when we stumble in sin, we will run to Him with confidence and sincere repentance instead of running from Him in condemnation and shame.

One of the ways that you start the process of building your identity in Jesus is by entering into a real interactive relationship with Him. First, you truly have to believe that Jesus loves you. You must choose to believe what the Bible says about who you are and who He is. Throughout the Bible, there are many verses that speak of God's love for us (see 1 John 4:7; John 14:21; Rom. 8:37; 2 Thess. 2:16). God is full of mercy and never-ending fathoms of love for His people.

God loves us so much that He sent His only Son to die so that we might be reconciled to Him (see John 3:16; Rom. 5:10; 2 Cor. 5:20). The Son whom God loved from before time was given for us so we could be close to God. Now, how beautiful and loving is that! Jesus died on the cross and rose from the dead because of love, not obligation.

It's not enough to know that Jesus loves you. You must believe that He loves you, and you must receive that love as well. Once you believe and receive, you will feel the confidence, strength, compassion, and sustaining power from your relationship. Part of the key to walking in all these truths is getting to a place where you can pull on the power of your relationship with the Father.

The reason that believing is so very important is this: If you do not believe that God loves you, then you have departed from the Faith. If you don't believe that God loves you with the same jealous, fiery, passionate, powerful love with which He loved Jesus, then you are shaking hands with false doctrine and idolatry.

We relate to God by the means which He has laid forth in His Word, on His terms, on the basis of who He is, who He says we are to Him, and how we are to relate to Him. The Spirit of Jesus the Son lives in us. Through His Son we build relationship with our Father in Heaven. The same confident love, privilege, and assurance that Jesus enjoyed are now offered freely to us as sons and daughters. Jesus even goes so far as to say that the love the Father has for Him is the same love the Father has for you and me. Yet, because of sin, lack of true repentance, and bad experiences and examples with natural fathers, it's not always easy to relate to God as our Father.

Nevertheless, the truth remains and beckons us to believe that God is our Father in Heaven. He's full of mercy, compassion, truth, power, and affection, and desires for our relationship with Him to be healthy and whole. We are called to be bold, confident sons and daughters that know who our Father is.

I remember a time when I was very wounded by a leader who was close to me. I respected and trusted this leader and I allowed him to have far too much control over my life. It is such a hard place to be in, to be balancing the ways you've failed, spiritual abuse, and rejection, all while walking out your faith. You say all sorts of things to yourself like, "I belong in this state of despair," and "I am just lucky to be here." Both of these statements are incredibly damaging. I remember one particular occasion when I was so overtaken with sorrow, all I could do was wish for this life to end. I begged God to love me in spite of my many failures, and for Him to help me through that process.

I tried to mend my heart and my situations on my own before I would let the Holy Spirit get into my wounds and do a powerful work in me. An important lesson I learned was that we can't be the Holy Spirit for ourselves or for anyone else.

In this difficult situation, I would lie to the abusive leader in my life by either making something up or taking the importance of something away, so the leader would think I was great or wouldn't think I was trying to be better than I was. I changed my experiences with God, both my successes and failures, based upon my identity in this leader. I learned through this season of rejection and pain that you cannot look to the source of your wound for help, but that you must look straight ahead into the burning eyes of the Father.

You see, understanding our identity in Christ is so important because it leads to our ultimate happiness and health. That matters to God. Oftentimes, we take our walk and gifting and distort them due to low self-esteem issues. We tell grandiose or exaggerated stories because we just can't believe ourselves special enough as we are. Or we hold back the wonderful testimonies in our lives based on low self-esteem and how an abusive leader has handled us.

During this time, the Lord did and said some amazingly beautiful things like, "I cry beside you, *not because of you.*" One moment the pain was so overwhelming that I thought I couldn't make it, and I literally wanted to die. While I was in this moment, I was caught up, and the Lord took me to an emergency room (which—if you knew my testimony—was a very meaningful place to me). After being a prodigal for seven years, I had a heart attack when I was 25. I had a heavenly encounter on an emergency room table, where I saw Jesus standing beside me holding my hand. My chest cavity was open wide and it looked like I had been in a terrible accident of some kind. Jesus put His hand on my face and locked eyes with me, then He said, "Don't look at the wound, sweetie. Don't look at it right now, OK? Papa is going to fix it…just don't look down right now, baby boy."

I had to learn to let Jesus love me and I had to believe that I loved Him as well. If I didn't believe, it would have been impossible to allow Him to do a deep work in me and I would not have made it through this critical and dangerous time in my life. Looking back, I suffered through loss of friendships and mentor relationships, false accusations, and a myriad of other forms of loss and pain. One of the immeasurably beautiful things about God is that, during all this pain, He was able to love me, and through His tender mercies, I came through the other side of this time with a faith that proved solid gold.

You see, if you come through the other side of your nightmare and you come out still believing, then your faith has been proven as honest and true. If you finish the race still loving Jesus and opening your heart to Him, you win in the end. For example, despite all King David's mistakes, at the end of his life, God said that David had done everything the Lord required of him. That is grace. That is mercy. That is God (see Acts 13:20-22).

One of the most glorious parts of our spiritual identity is that we are a new creation in Christ (see 2 Cor. 5:17). This is true of us because we received the gift of Jesus' righteousness, which is based on His finished work on the cross. We must learn to walk as believers in this fundamental basic foundation. We must walk in confidence with God, instead of in condemnation due to our past failures and trials (see Rom. 8:1).

Since we have been made a new creation in Christ Jesus, we are called to relate to God out of the righteousness of Christ Jesus that is already present in us. Most often, we relate to God out of a false sense of who we think we are. We attempt to hide what we believe is our true self (what we're ashamed of) from God, and stand before Him with a false self. We often feel all too close and connected to our most recent failures when relating to God. There is a difference between confessing before God that we have sinned and that we struggle, and taking on a shame-based identity before Him (see Rom. 6:13).

A problem that we can get into as people is that, through a lack of understanding and education, we can misinterpret immaturity as rebellion. The reason for this mislabeling is that on a surface level they both appear to be very similar. Many times, we can outwardly display an attitude or behavior that

can come off as rebellious when it's birthed out of immaturity. When we walk through rejection as it relates to our
identity, we can very easily take on an unhealthy identity
that is not the truth of who we are. We feel shamed and we
live out of that condemnation. When we are immature in
our identity, we must walk in grace and growth. We need to
be able to understand that our circumstances do not necessarily determine our motives and character. And current
circumstances may not be the result of correction or punishment for rebellion.

We can become very comfortable with judging the
motives of others, which I truly believe has gotten Christians
and the Church as a whole in a lot of trouble. I feel that
at times the Church can be too quick to judge, and way
too quick to form opinions. I think as Christians we have
too many opinions. God sees the heart, and we need to
pray that we would see others through the filter of the
Holy Spirit.

Here are some great questions that I have heard asked
in many church and ministry settings: How do you define
yourself? Do you define yourself by all the ways you have
struggled and missed the mark? Is your identity set up in the
fact that you sometimes fail? Or is your identity set up in the
truth that God loves you, in the truth that He has never been
ashamed of you or embarrassed to call you His own? Are you
a sinner who is a Christian, or are you a Christian who struggles with sin? We should define ourselves as Christians who
struggle but who are fully loved and cared for by the uncreated God of the universe whose affections are never-ending
toward us.

Being transformed into the likeness of Christ is a process. You don't all of a sudden become saved and then fully understand what it means to be righteous and holy. It takes time to make your faith your own. There are multiple steps to transformation. One of the first steps is having an honest desire to say no to sin. You may still struggle, but at least you have a *yes* in your heart before the Lord, and that is what will ultimately carry you through in the end.

We all struggle in our weakness. I remember hearing IHOP-KC mission leader Mike Bickle say in one of his sermons that the fact that our love is weak does not mean it is false love. A hypocrite is somebody who says one thing, but does not pursue it. A true lover of God does not attain everything that we sincerely pursue.

God has given the Church a wonderful opportunity to receive identity through intimacy with Him. If we do not experience identity through intimacy with Jesus, then our lives become weak in the Spirit. You see, the Holy Spirit activates the identity that God has spoken into us. We commune with the Holy Spirit, but the best communion comes from a dialogue where we are functioning out of our true identity.

We don't want to have a fake relationship with the Godhead. When we are not experiencing identity, when we are walking in obligation and not relation, then we are building on a relationship that is not aligned in strength and truth. This is part of the reason why people so easily get led astray and begin to build their identity on leaders and not on Jesus.

We have a major identity crisis in the Church. We have many people who will serve their pastor but who know very little of the character and nature of God. Basically we have people working in the temple but having no real connection with the Person who calls it home.

God's Affections for Us Establish Our Identity

The way that a child is raised will greatly affect their identity. Children largely are the products of their environments and upbringing. I know that as a child my natural father held me and sang over me. My earthly father showered his affections upon me and raised me up the best he knew how. My mother held me and sang over me as well (they were both hippies who received salvation during the Jesus People movement), and it was that kind of affection that helped to lay the foundation for the man I am today.

Likewise, it makes perfect sense that in order to know who you are in God, you must first experience His affections for you. There must be a time where you are loved into your identity in God. Jesus seriously desires to make this kind of connection with us. Jesus wants us to receive His affections for us and truly believe that they are genuine and without spite or malice (see Eph. 3:18-19).

When I felt my mother's and father's love and affection for me, my heart would come alive and I would feel as if I could do anything. This was also the same awareness that I felt when I failed or let them down. We often relate to God through the filters of our earthly relationships. This is something that is passed on to us at birth. It is designed by God because God wants us to relate to Him as our earthly father, and that is why it is wired into our very DNA to connect in this way.

When I felt my parents standing behind me 110 percent, I was empowered to chase my destiny. That is the very same reality in the Kingdom Covenant Relationship that God intended for us to live in. You see, when we connect with how God feels about us, we are empowered through the Holy Spirit to embrace our destiny and walk rightly with God, bearing much fruit. When we walk this very beautifully broken journey of life from the place of true identity, then we can take the storms that come our way. No matter the tragedy, sorrow, or testing, we will hold steady because our house (identity) is built upon the Rock. When we are confident in our self-esteem before God and man, then we have an easier time walking out humility and thus not wavering in the storms of life.

In previous sections you have heard me question where we take our pain. Well, I think it is most important to address the direction we are running when we are talking about identity. Do we run from God in our weakness or do we come to Him for our identity? We are dark yet lovely; but if we only see that we are dark, then we will never stick around to find out that we are also lovely. A healthy identity set up on God is the very fuel that fills us to run *to* Him instead of hiding *from* Him.

Like so many things in our lives, we need God's help to fulfill our end of the deal. We as a people are utterly and totally dependent on God's help to walk this out. The Word of God tells us that His ways are higher than our ways. Even the apostle Paul says, *"God's love passes knowledge"* (Eph. 3:19). We cannot walk out our identity without the revelatory gift of the Holy Spirit. We cannot love God without the help of the Holy Spirit; thus we cannot fully walk in the confidence of God's love (which produces identity) without the help of the Holy Spirit to make the divine connection.

With so many things talked about in our faith, we suffer from a spiritual eating disorder. We eat information and regurgitate it right back up before we have given the Holy Spirit time to mature the revelation within us. We tend to talk about all these really great ideas, and I myself have seen powerful speakers deliver life-changing messages to a roomful of people who will not do what it takes to experience it. I have given prophetic words that broke people (in a good way) and changed their circumstances, as well as witnessed powerful prophetic words given where everyone in the conference could not deny the presence of God in that place. Yet the people who were blessed and spoken to prophetically were not willing to take the direction or were not willing to do what it took to press into their destiny.

I feel like we have had this lack of motivation for so long that now it has spilled out of our mouths, down the pulpit, and into our communities, breeding a culture of false comfort and really great and comforting ideas about God, but with no transformation. We need to be a counter-culture and say *yes* to experiencing God's affections for us—all while letting it radically remake us as a people!

You know, it never seems to fail that the enemy will always assault the work of the Holy Spirit. Part of realizing who we are in relation to the Father is having clarity in the difference between the voice of the enemy and the voice of our Father. A good measuring tool for that is the Word of God. Diligence in prayer and reading the Word will implant within us a truth that can be breathed on by the Holy Spirit at the very moment we need it most.

You will know it's the enemy when whatever thought comes is based on accusation and not on correction in love. Correction from the Father is gentle and leaves us feeling able to succeed. On the other hand, accusation leaves us feeling defeated and broken. Satan is always trying to steal God's worship, and if he can do that by confusing us about our identity, then he has been successful in stealing that worship. I truly believe that one of the most power-ful forms of worship is choosing to believe who you are in Christ Jesus and relating to God out of that truth (see Rom. 8:32-39).

Having a real relationship can make people feel very uneasy. Sometimes we run from intimacy because we are afraid that we will fail or someone else will fail us. We become perfectionists and thus try to guard our hearts from God for fear that He will reject us if He truly sees us. The truth is that God already sees us deeper and in more truth and honesty than we see ourselves. Yet we fear that we will not be enough for God to love. It's no wonder that we find it difficult to have an intimate relationship with God when we are in constant fear of rejection and judgment.

The problem with being in fear of being rejected by God is that you are tormented with this idea that the other shoe will drop. You have to get to a place with God through intimacy where you know things will be OK. Even now I feel the Holy Spirit on me while I type this. God is not waiting for you to fail so He can reject you. The blood of Christ is stronger than that! To believe anything less is to agree with idolatry.

I personally struggle with the idea that the love and passion God has for Jesus is the same love and passion God feels for me. I have to remind myself, when I meet the disappointments of this life, that because Jesus was loved by the Father, then I am also loved by the Father. We are not second-class citizens, and God is not a hostage negotiator. Everything Jesus did on this earth (minus being crucified and paying for all the sins of all humankind) has been extended to us because Jesus now lives in us. To read the Word about the relationship between Jesus and God is to literally see the blueprint for our relationship.

I think too many Christians are afraid of doing wrong or messing up and losing the grace that has been set aside for them. We tend to treat our relationship with God as if we were on a tight rope. We must walk just so or we will plummet to the ground and be lost forever. I promise you that this is not Christianity.

> *Therefore, if anyone is in Christ, he is a new creation;* ***old things have passed away;*** *behold,* ***all things*** *have become new. Now* ***all things*** *are of God, who has reconciled us to Himself through Jesus…that is, that God was in Christ reconciling the world to Himself,* ***not imputing their trespasses to them***.… *For He made Him* [Jesus] *who knew no sin to be sin for us,* ***that we might***

become the righteousness of God *in Him* (2 Corinthians 5:17-19;21 NKJV, Emphasis added).

When you are confident in a relationship, you are not afraid of being rejected or of being judged. I know that I can go to my wife or my parents with anything and that they will love me through it. I am confident in love. God is trying to get us to that place where we trust Him. We need to arrive at the understanding that He is not waiting to reject us but is waiting to love on us.

The Word says that *"perfect love casts out all fear"* (1 John 4:18), which is a pretty great tool for measuring not only your earthly relationships, but also your covenant relationship with the Father. We are supposed to grow in understanding and maturity as it relates to the different levels of God's character and nature. When we understand His love, we will not fear Him or the relationship that He is beckoning us to.

The beauty of love is this: as we enter into a relationship that blooms into love, all of sudden we start making choices out of love. For example, I know that since my wedding, my love for my wife has transformed and grown into an altogether new type of desire and love. I make choices out of the place of love and not out of obligation. This is how we are to live in relationship with the Father. We are progressively transformed by love, and our desire to pursue holiness is breathed upon by that loving relationship.

Do you want someone to make the right choices out of obligation or duty, or from the place of love? Ultimately, when you are controlled by love, then making choices out of that love is a natural reflex. In this way, we are transformed progressively by the revelation of God's love and affection.

In our human relationships, most of the time we wait for someone to show us that they like us first before we are willing to take the next step. Oftentimes, we look for some kind of signal, some kind of hint that we are adored. We take whatever we can get as a clue and we unabashedly run with it. Many people wonder if God even loves them. People are searching for love and have not been told that God is crazy in love with them!

The beauty of this romance with God is that you don't have to guess if you are loved. The Word tells us in First John 4:19 that God loved us first. This means God is showing His hand to all of humanity. God is saying, "You are already loved; now just agree with the truth and love Me back." This is the very place that we derive the power of identity from—in the place of truth and love. It is the revelation that we are loved that begets love. When we believe and choose to understand the character and nature of God's love, we are given the strength to run back to God.

Whatever we encounter about God's heart (His passion) for us becomes awakened in our heart back to God. Encounter (meditation unto revelation) results in transformation. What we understand about God's heart is essential to transforming our emotions. We change our mind, and then God changes our hearts. We change our mind (understanding about God), then God changes our emotions (unlocks our hearts). Wrong understanding about God damages our hearts. Wrong ideas about God's personality leads to blocking our intimacy with Him.

Walking on the Water

When Jesus fed the 5,000, He showed Himself greater than a human magician who could just heal some individuals or turn some stones into bread. This I feel was one of the major themes of Jesus' life on earth: He wanted to correct the misunderstanding of what the Messiah was truly meant to embody. Jesus turned the religious culture of His time on its ear. For instance, when He walked on the sea (see Matt. 14:22-36), Jesus was doing something that the Hebrew Bible had reserved for God alone (see Job 9:8; Ps. 77:19; Hab. 3:15). Nevertheless, as in an earlier storm scene (see Matt. 8:23-27), Matthew is interested here in teaching us not only Christology but also about the essential faith for disciples (see Matt. 8:26). Of all the disciples, Peter alone begins to walk on the water, but Jesus regards even his faith as less than what a disciple should have.

> *Immediately He made the disciples get into the boat and go ahead of Him to the other side, while He dismissed the crowds. After dismissing the crowds, He went up on the mountain by Himself to pray. When evening came, He was there alone. But the boat was already over a mile from land, battered by the waves, because the wind was against them. Around three in the morning, He came toward them walking on the sea. When the disciples saw Him walking on the sea, they were terrified. "It's a ghost!" they said, and cried out in fear. Immediately Jesus spoke to them. "Have courage! It is I. Don't be*

afraid." "Lord, if it's You," Peter answered Him, "command me to come to You on the water." "Come!" He said. And climbing out of the boat, Peter started walking on the water and came toward Jesus. But when he saw the strength of the wind, he was afraid. And beginning to sink he cried out, "Lord, save me!" Immediately Jesus reached out His hand, caught hold of him, and said to him, "You of little faith, why did you doubt?" When they got into the boat, the wind ceased. Then those in the boat worshiped Him and said, "Truly You are the Son of God!" (Matthew 14:22-33 HCSB).

I truly believe that when Jesus spoke to Peter and said, *"Oh you of little faith,"* He was saying to Peter primarily this: "Peter, why do you not have faith in your ability to follow Me?"

This is also a vital scenario that is being played out right now in the personal lives of the saints. Jesus is calling us out of our boats in faith, and through the filters of what we know, we doubt our ability to follow Him.

There are times that we wrestle with the Lord and not with satan. We cannot blame every discomfort on the enemy, but we must understand that testing from the Lord is producing all sorts of godly character. Here is how the *Matthew Henry Commentary* explains this scenario:

Jesus' Coming Should Bring an End to Fear

If the disciples were still struggling against the winds at the fourth watch of the night—the

59

Romans divided the night into four instead of the Jewish three watches—the disciples must have been exhausted. Probably accustomed to awakening around 6:00 A.M., they instead found themselves still trying to cross the lake between 3:00 and 6:00 A.M. We may scoff at the disciples for accepting the popular notion of ghosts, but the biggest offense here is that they still underestimate Jesus' power. It has not occurred to them that he could know their circumstances, walk on water to come to them or catch up to them in a storm! To their credit, however, the fear issue seems to be solved once they recognize that their teacher is with them. They knew him well enough to know that if he were there, he would bring them through their storm.[1]

Do we trust the goodness of God? Do we truly believe that He has good thoughts and plans for our lives?

Sometimes I imagine God trying to interact with us on earth, and when He draws near, we flinch and shrink back, convinced that His goodness is really punishment. Oftentimes, we seem like wounded animals in a trap, and we are convinced that the Lord's desire to set us free is somehow connected to our painful circumstance. The *Matthew Henry Commentary* continues:

Jesus Wants Us to Imitate His Works

Although the proposal that Peter walk on water is first Peter's idea (v. 28), Jesus' response indicates that he approves of it (v. 29). Peter is gently reproved not for presumptuously stepping from the boat but for presumptuously doubting in the very presence of Jesus (v. 31; compare 6:30; 8:26; 16:8; 17:20…). Disciples were expected to imitate their masters, and Jesus is training disciples who will not simply regurgitate his oral teachings but will have the faith to demonstrate his authority in practice as well.[2]

Once Jesus has given the command, walking on water is simply a matter of trusting the One who has performed so many miracles in the past. Peter's failure comes as he observes the wind (see Matt. 14:30), looking to his situation rather than to God's power that is sustaining him. Still, Peter knows by this point whom to cry out to; his feeble attempt to walk on water is no more feeble than our first attempts to walk on land. Our faith may be more infantile than Peter's if we have never even tried to step out in obedience to Jesus' commands or direction for our lives; many of us have less practice walking in faith than two-year-olds have walking physically.

It is important to note that while Jesus is disappointed with Peter's inadequate faith, Peter has acted in greater faith than the other disciples—he is learning. Faith cannot be worked up by formulas or emotion, but it grows through various tests as we continue to trust our Lord and He continues to teach us. Faith grows out of a relationship with the Person of Jesus, and in no other way.

Questions

1. Do you feel like you have low self-esteem?

2. What does the Bible say about who you are?

3. Are you using boundaries as an excuse to keep others out?

4. Do you believe that God loves you?

5. Do you believe that God loves you with the same love that He has for Jesus?

6. Think about walking on water. Do you believe that God has given you what you need to be successful?

7. What is it about yourself that you find inadequate?

8. Why is it that you are afraid to try to be successful?

Endnotes

1.	Matthew Henry's Commentary, Matthew 14:25-27, http://www.biblegateway.com/resources/commentaries/IVP-NT/Matt/Lord-Sea.

2.	Ibid., Matthew 14:28-31.

FOUNDATIONS FOR PRAYER

*The Word gives us the instructions
and the Holy Spirit gives us the ability.*

The Body of Christ is in great need of diligence when it comes to self-government as it pertains to reading and applying the Word of God and prayer. How will you know what is expected of you unless you get informed on it… unless you search it out? How will you know you have been successful if you don't know what success looks like? How will you allow the Holy Spirit to correct you to get you back on course when your theology is off base? Usually, when ministries and individuals are not grounded in the Word, they become eccentric and their view of God becomes perverted. You see, it's not enough to just say a prayer; you must cultivate maturity in the knowledge of God. This requires time in the Word to get the revelation of who God is and what our role is in this whole drama that is being played out.

> *But now He has reconciled you by His physical body through His death, to present you holy, faultless, and blameless before Him—if indeed you remain grounded and steadfast in the faith, and are not shifted away from the hope of the gospel that you heard. [This gospel] has been proclaimed in all creation under heaven, and I, Paul, have become a minister of it* (Colossians 1:22-23 HCSB).

One day in prayer I was just talking with the Holy Spirit and I asked, "Why does it seem like the Church as a whole is lacking so much character? Why is it that I read the Word and realize I am not producing the type of fruit that is expected of me?"

It is due to a lack of vision! A people without knowledge perish (see Prov. 29:18). Churches are dying off in great numbers due to lack of knowledge. It's as if we say *yes* to the gift of salvation but then don't put energy into maturing into what we are called to be.

This same day I was talking with the Holy Spirit, the comment came to me: "Most people pray the prayer, but I don't really hear from them after that." This was so heartbreaking to ponder on. Did you know that 80 percent of Christian high school students fall away from the Church after graduation? We as the Church must get educated and step up to the plate and disciple the new believers and those who are weak. We need to encourage them to grow and to make their faith their own in order to help produce some honesty and longevity in their walk.

However, I believe there are two main reasons we don't like to mentor people. The first is that we don't feel educated enough ourselves. We feel like we won't have the answers and that we will look uneducated. This is the very reason we *must* take up this call! *Iron sharpens iron* (Prov. 27:17). The other reason I believe we struggle in mentoring others is due to the fact that it requires personal sacrifice.

> *My people are destroyed for lack of knowledge.*
> *Because you have rejected knowledge, I also will*
> *reject you from being priest for Me; because you*
> *have forgotten the law of your God, I also will*
> *forget your children* (Hosea 4:6 NKJV).

We can read all of the great things the Bible has to say about godliness and living a life set apart for the Gospel, but if we do not rely on prayer and the power of the Holy Spirit to enable us, we are not going to make it! For years, people in the church have tried under their own strength to strive for godliness, only to wind up empty and religious. We cannot achieve godly character through religious obligation; we must be motivated by the power of the Holy Spirit. God is looking for those who are gripped by love and leaning on the Holy Spirit for what they need.

We cannot worship God without His help; we cannot even love God without God giving us the ability through the Holy Spirit to do so.

There are promises of God in the Word that the Holy Spirit is just waiting to activate in our own lives! I believe that the Holy Spirit literally activates the Word in us! That it becomes a fire shut up in our bones!

The promise to do greater works—to walk on water, to move mountains—is, I believe, just waiting to be activated by the Holy Spirit.

How does the Holy Spirit activate what's inside us? Prayer and spending time in the Word are the simple but difficult answers to this question.

Empowering Prayer

Prayer is a fundamental, living, active necessity in our relationship with God.

Prayer is where a holy God draws near. God wants to communicate because He *is* personal. We pray to a God who longs to reveal Himself.

The attributes of a life of prayer cannot be hidden; they will manifest in ways that people see. These ways are not always big in the natural, but are huge in the supernatural.

Effective prayer must be grounded in the Word. I believe there are nine fundamental elements to a lifestyle of empowering prayer. When I say *empowering prayer*, I am speaking of prayer that empowers us as the reader.

Faith: You must trust God. Prayer is pointless if you don't think God can or will hear your prayer. Also, if you believe that God won't do anything, then you are missing the major point of prayer and the heart of the Father.

Adoration: God is love and He desires us to worship Him with our whole being (see Matt. 22:37). Our love should be expressed to God! God has shown us His love in deeds and in the Word. God has said and shown us His love and desires a response from weak human vessels.

Worship: In worship, we get to give adoration to God and get our eyes off ourselves. This is why faith in God's promises and character is so very important to our lives. We must trust that we are forgiven, and come before Him with thanksgiving in worship. The enemy also wants our worship; and if he can get us looking inward, then we can't worship God. We end up worshiping our problems—and thus satan robs God of His worship. We must have our eyes fixed on Jesus instead of on our problems and what we fear (after all, we tend to worship what we fear).

Praise: We speak well of those we love and respect. Because we should love God the most, He should get the highest praise. Christians should talk more about the excellencies of Christ! We should speak of Him often and with great passion!

Confession: A confrontation with the Holy Spirit leads us to the conviction of our own sin (see 1 John 1:9). We need to confess what we did as a sin before God, the only One who is able to forgive us. We must also trust God with what we've done.

Dedicated Action: Prayer founded in the reality of Christ should not cause us to lose our personalities, nor should it cause us to become hermits or withdraw from society or the Church. We should not consider ourselves greater than the Church. A critical spirit is not a sign of dedication and great spirituality. Rather, dedication and prayer should produce in us a desire to serve those around us. Authentic prayer will produce courage and productivity.

Request: Prayer is not just a way to respond to God. Prayer is also a way to ask for God's provision for ourselves and others. Our wrong motives in prayer are sometimes the reason that God will not hear our petition. We can always ask the Father, but we must have the right motives. When we are in agreement with God, He will hear our petition! Prayer is a request to a personal God who answers as He feels is best. God knows us best and He knows the fullness of what we truly need.

Effectiveness: Prayer has power over everything! God can act intelligently in any part of the universe or human history. Although people may think what we do is foolish, the Bible says that *"the effective, fervent prayer of a righteous man avails much"* (James 5:16 NKJV). Biblical history shows us that prayer can change nature and physical bodies. Our prayers make a difference in how God acts in the world (see Acts 4:31; Jon. 2:7-10; James 5:17-18).

Fasting: Fasting is voluntarily going without legitimate pleasures. Its purpose is getting closer to the fire, so to speak. An interesting aspect of fasting is what it can bring to the surface. When you are fasting, what controls you comes to the surface. But God is not overly impressed with our ability to fast. It is for *our* benefit! When we fast, we become weak; but it's a safe place of self-revelation in Jesus Christ. Jesus is fasting in Heaven! Jesus didn't say *if* you fast; He said *when* you fast (see Matt. 6:17). Fasting is very important for the sake of sensitivity, spirituality, and as an important part of prayer.

Let us grasp these tools to produce a personal maturity within ourselves, and as a community of believers move forward in saying *yes* to the empowering strength of the Holy Spirit, who gives us the ability to use these tools as we pursue excellence in character.

 Questions

1. Are you dialoguing and building a communication-based relationship with the Holy Spirit?

2. Are you giving the Holy Spirit something to work with?

3. As humans, we are always bringing forth and producing. What are you bringing forth? What are you planting and producing?

CYCLES OF COMMUNITY

Every community goes through prosperous times and difficult periods. Also, communities can be created, they can age, and they can die just like living organisms. However, the obvious difference is that communities are not automatically destined to die. Often, the actions of the residents in a community will either give it life or cause it to die.

Communities in general have four basic cycles. These four cycles are not necessarily the progression in every case. The cycles of community are the Delivery Phase, the Expansion Phase, the Inactivity Phase, and the Stability Phase. We will go over these four cycles to gain a better understanding and to get equipped with the tools for building a community that will last and bear much fruit.

The first cycle is the *Delivery Phase*. The delivery phase is the birth period or origin of a community. Usually, the delivery phase is associated with an event that gives a ministry community its original call or identity. Many communities have a story about what caused them to come forward and start the ministry or church. That is such a beautiful thing to me—the idea that every church or ministry has a unique qualifier that thrusts them into a movement.

The second cycle is the *Expansion Phase*. This step in the process must be internally driven. Those who live in a church or ministry community are personally vested into the ministry by way of finances, emotional support, physical support, spiritual support, and social support. The resulting efforts lead to further expansion of all facets of the ministry community.

The third cycle is the *Inactivity Phase*. This phase creates sleepless nights for pastors and ministry leaders. The Inactivity Phase is when the driving and growing force behind the Expansion Phase has failed in thrusting the ministry community forward. Sometimes this stagnation can appear to be a period of stability, and that's why communication is such an important element for all levels of leadership to embrace. By communicating, you can determine if the driving force behind a movement has stopped and thus is producing stagnation, or if the level of support is healthy and thus is stabilizing the ministry community.

The fourth cycle is the *Stability Phase*. This phase of vitality is when the community has become self-sufficient in regard to financial responsibility, equipping, and responsibility. This phase is not necessarily marked with huge growth or prosperity. Vitality in this phase means a progressive stability within the ministry community. In this cycle of community, the leadership is pulling its weight as well as doing periodic social and spiritual community maintenance.

Disarming the Monster: Healthy Community

In this section we will discuss what it looks like to live in a community that is healthy. When we speak of *healthy,* we do not mean a community that is perfect. It would be unfair to expect any ministry or church that we are a part of to be perfect. We need to extend grace as much as we desperately need it ourselves.

I feel that five basic freedoms are necessary in order to produce a safe and healthy community in any ministry or church setting. This list of five elements is not all-inclusive, but I have found them to be good indicators of whether or not you are in a healthy community. The five freedoms are:

1. Freedom to fail.

2. Freedom to feel.

3. Freedom to be corrected in love.

4. Freedom of relationship.

5. Freedom to be restored.

This list of five freedoms is a positive checklist that church leaders as well as those attending can use to evaluate themselves. You need to ask, "Are we providing these things?" or "Am I feeling these as part of my environment here?"

The first of the five freedoms is the ***freedom to fail.*** We must be willing to love one another through our shortcomings and failures. We as a church or ministry community must anticipate the fact that those we love will at times miss the mark. It is when we get too deep into other's lives that we become their masters and drive them as slaves to perform and never make a mistake. We become those who attempt to control their sin, and in doing so, we break their spirits. Many people will question this freedom, so I will answer their concerns before I get letters in the mail…No, this does not give us an excuse to be OK with unrighteousness, nor does it give us license to give up on the pursuit of godly character.

The second freedom is the *freedom to feel.* We must provide a healthy environment for everyone in community to embrace the fullness of their personalities and emotions. For too long, people in church and ministry communities have suppressed their desire to experience pleasure. Unfortunately, at a moment of weakness, this natural desire created by God can boil over into sin. We need to encourage others to be real with God about what they are feeling. We should not become performance-based in our relationship with the Father and thus negate the grace allotted to us by God (see Jonah 2:8). In the realm of a redeemed heart, our emotions can be a powerful way of experiencing and communing with God.

The third element in this list is *freedom to be corrected in love.* We must not be afraid in the name of grace to correct our fellow believers in love (see Gal. 6:1). The Word gives us a list of godly characteristics that are expected of us as we grow in the Lord (see 2 Cor. 6:3-10). Church leadership has a responsibility to equip the community as well as to call its members to a higher place of character. It is when we struggle to control others that this process turns into abuse. Love must be the primary motivation behind the need to correct someone within our community or church. The ultimate outcome of being corrected in love is maturity.

The fourth element is *freedom of relationship.* Enabling people to own their relationship with the Lord is a beautiful gift. We should encourage each individual to embrace who Christ is as well as who they are in Christ. We do not want to create a codependent church. We don't want people from the church coming to you as a leader and asking questions like, "What kind of car should I buy?" or "Who should I marry?" These are questions that are reserved for the Lord first and foremost. Yes, it is true that prophecy should confirm what the Lord has already told them, but it can't replace the direction or voice of God for that individual. We must allow the individual to be led by the Holy Spirit, and remember that we ourselves cannot become the Holy Spirit for others. We need to get out of the way and learn to trust the Holy Spirit in others.

The final element in this list is *freedom to be restored.* This is a tricky area for most churches and ministries. The main question is, where is the dividing line between immaturity and a lack of desire for righteousness? Repentance is the starting point for all avenues of restoration. When someone is repentant, it does not mean that they are begging God or us for forgiveness. Repentance literally means to change your mind or change your behavior. Oftentimes, people fool themselves into thinking that admitting they have fallen short or sinned is the same as being forgiven, but it is not. Admitting that you have done something wrong is not the same as asking for forgiveness and changing your ways. Plenty of people can say, "Yes, that was wrong," but that doesn't mean they have changed their behavior. Leadership must address the behavior behind the sin; they must not let restoration rest solely on hoops that need to be jumped through. Leadership has a greater responsibility to walk the individual who is being restored back to wholeness in Jesus. Being reconciled to God is more important than proving how sorry you are.

We read in the Bible where it says, *"Be careful restoring a brother so you yourself don't fall"* (Gal. 6:1). This Scripture gets twisted in the minds of those who read it. Oftentimes, someone will say that it means you should be aggressive when restoring someone so you don't fall into the same sin they did. But I believe that the Scripture is actually stating this: Don't fall into sin by breaking their spirit and judging the one you are restoring. The Scripture gives you the idea that the individual has already been found acceptable to be restored, so it's no longer an issue of repentance. Peter denied Christ three times, then was restored and a week later Peter's shadow was healing people. I think most ministry communities and churches do not have a healthy grid for walking out other's restoration. This is a very good example that Jesus gave us in (see John 21:15-19).

Churches as well as ministries have an obligation and a privilege to establish people's identities as Christians through the teaching of the Word, as well as directing them to the nature and character of God. I want to encourage those around me to have a healthy self-esteem and a healthy mental outlook of themselves as a beautiful creation and as an image bearer. We have been made a new creation in Christ Jesus! This radically remakes us. People need to know that God is in love with them. We need to know that we as the human race are not only just lucky to be here, but also that God wanted us in the equation.

A healthy community is any community that does its best both corporately and privately to present an accurate picture of the character and attributes of God. The leadership of any ministry community or church community must enable the wider Body of Christ to have a healthy perspective on its relationship with God. God has often been misrepresented, and it is our job to align ourselves with God in the Spirit of Truth and bring forth the correct image as best as we humanly can.

We must be diligent in our portrayal of this relationship. We must give an accurate picture of what grace is and what it means. Some people who have been abused and rejected find themselves on one of two sides of the extreme. They either find themselves not willing to extend grace to others, or they think that godly character is based on the human compass of guilt rather than on the Holy Spirit.

Oftentimes, I think we struggle with giving grace to others because we fear it makes us less special. We like to allow grace for the areas of darkness or immaturity in our own lives, but we don't want to reach out to others with the same understanding. We are afraid to let anyone else be special to God. I believe that part of the reason we feel this way is that we think, "If everyone is special, then *no one* is." This is a very misguided and broken understanding of the awesome omnipotence of God's ability to extend Himself fully to all humanity. We need to remember that God is quite capable of loving every one of us as if we were each the apple of His eye. And if we want to be a part of creating a healthy church or ministry community, we need to encourage and promote the five freedoms, both in ourselves and in others.

Questions

1. Do you confuse living in a healthy community with perfection?

2. Does your community provide the five basic freedoms necessary for a healthy community? If not, what is missing from your community?

3. Are you being proactive in helping to create a healthy culture for yourself?

4. As a ministry or even simply as a Christian, are you pointing others to Christ instead of to yourself?

Chapter 5

BEING A SAFE PLACE

One of the beautiful things that the Lord provides for us is a place where we can be safe. We don't often relate to God this way, but it is a biblical, theological truth that God is a safe place for us. In Him, we are safe to succeed, be upset, be wrong, or fail. This is the very nature that we need to emulate in our culture. We are called to make the church—as individuals and as a community—a safe place.

As we build community, we must keep in mind that others in our communities will fail. A lasting community is a community that anticipates failure, and in this reality has a plan in place that provides a healthy restoration process—for those times when restoration is needed. It is when we create a culture that produces performance-based and negative striving in community, that we lay a foundation for broken-ness and rejection.

When we establish a culture that gives the impression that the leadership is above reproach, then we are really establishing a hiddenness in our community. In this type of church culture, people become convinced that others have all the answers, and do not struggle with the same things they struggle with. Thus, those who are hurting and struggling in sin become even more withdrawn, and they live in hiddenness. The major problem of withdrawing into hiddenness is that it drives the sliver of a sinful lifestyle deeper into your soul.

I cannot tell you the countless number of people who have written to me or come to me for counseling who have dealt with shame and hiddenness in their marriages, private lives, and church communities. The number of beautifully broken Christians would astound you. Many in the Church and in ministry communities are in a very real war inside themselves over issues in their lives.

Communities receive part or most of their identities through the mass perception of the ministry leadership. This is why we must teach in community the importance of being a safe place for others.

Oftentimes, people don't confess one to another, due to their fear of exposure and rejection. Many people have shared with me their stories concerning confession and community. I remember one story where the confession process went something like this: "I made a mistake and I viewed some pornography. It has been years since I looked at that stuff, but I guess I was weak…?" Then the friend in the ministry community to whom this person confessed went to the direct leader to tell what was just told to them. This young man was then removed from his ministry community over a one-time offense. Now, I realize this was an extreme case, but I have heard many stories where the only lesson the broken person learned was, "Hey, if you screw up, don't confess, because it's not safe," or "Stay hidden and pretend everything is OK."

A responsible leader will help to create a community that walks others through healing, confession, forgiveness, and restoration. This is still a very sensitive area for most churches and ministry communities. I think part of the reason the Church gets so caught up in this issue is because they are afraid of being accused of letting their members take advantage of grace. Well, there is a huge difference between immaturity and giving in to a sinful lifestyle.

A Safe Place...to Fail or to Succeed

Being a safe place doesn't mean being just a safe place to fail. Being a safe place also means being a safe place to succeed. We need to encourage our people to grow and mature into the Bride of Christ that they are called to be. Most people struggle with their issues partly due to lack of knowledge and maturity. I truly believe that the number of straight up rebellious believers is a far smaller number than the number of those who are simply uneducated and immature.

An important lesson for the Body to learn is the difference between righteousness and holiness. Oftentimes, when people become believers, they think, "I am holy because Christ lives in me." But holiness is not something that is imparted automatically at the point of salvation. We become righteous instantaneously when we accept Jesus Christ as our personal

Savior, but at that point we get to *pursue* holiness because of the grace that has come through Jesus Christ. Grace enables us to pursue holiness and attain it! Throughout the New Testament, Scriptures speak of pursuing godly character and being holy (see Rom. 5:3-5; 2 Cor. 7:1; Eph. 4:24).

Being a safe place to succeed means having a level of excellence in our teaching and in our general understanding of the character and nature of God. As a leadership team, we must set people up for success. We must give the congregation the tools and education to understand and build a foundationally strong relationship with God.

One of the greatest tools to help people succeed is to build up their identities in Christ Jesus. If we want our people to be healthy and to reach for the stars, then we must instill in them a true hunger for the revelation of Jesus, and let that be their compass. We will not be disappointed in the fruit that will come as a result.

Questions

1. Are you living in hiddenness?

2. Are you OK with admitting that you fail?

3. Is your perception lined up with truth?

4. Think back to when you were a baby Christian. With the knowledge you have now, would you be hard on that baby Christian? Would you confuse immaturity for rebellion?

THE CHURCH WALKING DIFFERENTLY

I have been hearing many reports from other ministries and friends who are finding themselves in a deep struggle as of late. They feel caught up in difficulties economically, spiritually, and personally. I have also noticed in my own life over this time period a measure of straining, testing, and breakthrough in personal and spiritual issues. It has been very exhausting for many people, and some have even left the ministry or are beginning to fold up their tents, so to speak, and retire. It has become increasingly hard for certain individuals and ministries to function in a prosperous way or find a sustainable measure of breakthrough.

These struggles brought me to prayer and the Word of God where I found myself reading, pondering, arguing, laughing, and eventually getting a prophetic download from the Holy Spirit. I was searching and asking, "Lord, what is going on here? Why are things so tough right now? What is the major issue? What are You after?"

The Holy Spirit said one phrase to me that I believe unlocks a strategic view for the Church as well as for myself in this season of hardship. The Spirit said, "This is the twofold season of Jacob." The moment the Holy Spirit spoke those words to me, I felt something mighty hit my spirit! The Holy Spirit said that the twofold seasons of Jacob are the seasons of "wrestling" and of "Jacob's ladder." The Holy Spirit took me to two very specific Scriptures in the Word concerning Jacob (see Gen. 32:24-31; Gen. 28:12).

Often we think it is the enemy that is slowing us down, when really it is the Lord testing us and building our character! It is the Lord Himself trying to do a good work within us, making our faith as pure gold! I felt the Holy Spirit say, "Don't stop wrestling with God!" People are giving up on the journey of character development, both personally and corporately, due to a major misunderstanding of what God is doing. We are going to miss this great work of producing wisdom and perseverance if we dismiss this testing as demonic oppression.

The enemy has a plan to destroy the Church and this *now move* of God. Now is the time, and this generation must learn to decipher what is oppression and what is testing of character. The Lord is going to give us wisdom from the Holy Spirit so we don't lose momentum on this journey to major breakthrough!

This generation is being given a specific opportunity for openness and authenticity before the uncreated God of the universe! This generation is wrestling with God, and in this process, God Himself is training us to wrestle. God is teaching us to be strong and to have endurance, perseverance, and steadfastness. This generation will receive a reversal of seasons. Just as Jacob first had the dream of Jacob's ladder and later wrestled with God, this generation will wrestle with God and receive a breakthrough, and it will open Jacob's ladder. The breakthrough that is coming is literally the heavens being opened! Angels ascending and descending! God is dedicated to bringing large-scale breakthrough in personal lives, churches, and regions through our intimacy with Him and diligence in prayer.

As we say *yes* to God and allow Him to produce character in us, we will come into agreement with where He is taking us. God is looking for a generation who will be a *container for the times*. God is looking for a generation who will allow the old wineskin to be broken—a generation who will rise in a confidant relationship with the Father and stand in strength!

After his wrestling match with the Angel of the Lord, Jacob walked with a limp; and the Holy Spirit said, "That is what I am looking for. I am looking for a Church and a new generation who will come out leaning on her Beloved." The Holy Spirit said, "I am looking for a Church and a generation who will walk differently." People could look at Jacob after that point and tell that he walked differently after his heavenly contending encounter. That is what God is after in this *now move*, a generation motivated by intimacy and a desire to walk it out differently. God wants a generation who longs to see Him face to face!

Jacob then named the place Peniel, "For," [he said,] "I have seen God face to face, and I have been delivered." The sun shone on him as he passed by Peniel—limping on his hip (Genesis 32:30 HCSB).

The season of Jacob's ladder is the season of an open Heaven. During this season, the Lord is going to be opening the heavens in a mighty way, and that literally is the breakthrough. The breaking is Heaven itself responding to the diligence of prayer and the steadfastness of God's people. This is a time when those who have been tested and tried and found full of love and faith will be "accelerated" in the Body of Christ.

There is a generation that the spirit of religion has tried to abort! This false spirit of religion is standing in the midst of the Church and saying to a new generation, "You don't belong here." And the Holy Spirit is looking for a people and a generation who will stand up in the Church and say, "Get out" to this spirit of religion. God desires a generation who will fight for the birth of this movement!

The place at which Jacob stopped for the night and had his heavenly encounter was Mount Moriah, the future home of the Temple in Jerusalem. The ladder therefore signifies the "bridge" between Heaven and earth, as prayers and sacrifices offered in the Holy Temple provided a connection between God and the Jewish people. Moreover, the ladder alludes to the Giving of the Torah as another connection between Heaven and earth.

God is going to pour out His Spirit in geographic regions and churches. The Lord is looking for a place to call home.

The Lord is saying, "Who will build a house for Me, and where can I find rest?" In His message to me about the twofold seasons of Jacob, the Holy Spirit was saying that if people set themselves aside to do things differently and co-labor with the Lord, He will build a bridge between Heaven and earth!

In John 1:51, there is a clear reference to Jacob's dream (see Gen. 28:12), and it points toward Jesus Christ, who is called by His title, the Son of Man:

> *And He said to him, "Truly, truly, I say to you, you will see heaven opened, and the angels of God ascending and descending on the Son of Man."*

That is, by *"the angels of God ascending and descending,"* a perpetual divine interaction should now be opened between Heaven and earth, through the medium of Christ, who was God manifested in the flesh. Our blessed Lord is represented in His mediatory capacity as the Ambassador of God to men. The angels *"ascending and descending on the Son of Man"* is a metaphor taken from the custom of dispatching couriers or messengers from the prince to his ambassador in a foreign court, and from the ambassador back to the prince. The breakthrough is coming!

Questions

1. Are you inviting the Lord to test your character?

2. Do you know the difference between testing and oppression?

3. What are you doing to be a container for the times?

CARRIERS OF THE KINGDOM OF LOVE

The Holy Spirit has been speaking to me about us being carriers of the Kingdom of Love to the world around us—that we the Church could succeed in loving others to a place of breakthrough and a healthy relationship with the Father and with the Church. Within each one of us who are born again lives the Kingdom. We have Jesus living inside of us. The word *Christian* actually means "little Christ." This was a term that early Hasidic Jews and pagans used in a slanderous way to speak of those who followed Jesus. The name came about because of the desire that believers had to follow Jesus when Jesus was not looked upon in high regard in most of the social circles of His day.

The world does not understand the economy of the Kingdom, and the world didn't understand the followers of

Christ or what they were seeing in Jesus. The Kingdom of Heaven is an upside-down, inside-out Kingdom where you lose to gain (see Matt. 10:39; Matt. 16:25). Jesus was a Revolutionary with ideas that pushed the religious leaders of His day to the brink and eventually over the brink to His crucifixion.

When approaching healing, deliverance, prophetic words, teaching, preaching, and evangelism, it does us good to be reminded that we can do all things because Jesus lives in us and gives us strength (see Eph. 3:16). The Holy Spirit gives us the ability to do and think as Jesus did and thought. The Holy Spirit literally activates the promises of God in us! We are co-heirs in Christ, and because of Jesus, we have the ability to function like Christ. We can heal, cast out demons, grow in understanding and maturity, and show compassion. Jesus didn't do anything that we can't do—other than pay the debt of all of humankind through the crucifixion.

The Holy Spirit asked me the question: "Where are you taking Jesus and what are you doing with Him?" Are we operating in the Kingdom in a positive way? We can either take the Jesus in us into heavenly things or we can take Him into the place of shaking hands with darkness. Which one are we doing?

In First Corinthians 6:12-20, Paul clearly says that we should not sin against our body because we are joined in Spirit with Jesus. Paul asks a question of us that I skimmed by at first, but then decided to look back into a little further. First Corinthians 6:15 says,

> *Do you not know that your bodies are members of Christ? Shall I then take the members* [or

parts] *of Christ and make them members of a prostitute? Never!*

This idea began to race through my mind in this way: Every time I choose to do something that is not out of love or faith, I am taking a part of Jesus with me. It also means that I become susceptible to the power of the enemy. When I give the enemy legal right to be in an area of my life, I take away the legal right of the Father to protect me in those areas—thus providing a foothold for the enemy.

We have the free will to operate in godly character or to choose sin. It's not about God leaving us or not being strong enough, but it is about us choosing to create distance on our end between God and us.

Asking the questions concerning our character will hopefully push us into a place of grace and wholehearted aspiration for godly character. I am constantly being presented with the idea that we need to call upon the power of our relationship with Jesus to be successful in overcoming and being doers of the Kingdom. Jesus called upon His relationship with the Father, and that is the place the Kingdom was expanded from. It wasn't just because Jesus was fully God and fully man. Jesus never called upon His divinity to heal, cast out demons, or love someone. He called upon the loving relationship He had with His Father.

Jesus was the perfect example walked out before us on how to make it as a carrier of the Kingdom of Love. Jesus modeled it perfectly in the Word for us so we could make it! We were not given something we couldn't understand. We were given something that was attainable: a loving relationship with the Father. Through that relationship, we have the ability to walk out the Kingdom in Love.

Let love dictate where and how you carry the Kingdom. Not because of religious obligation, but because of love we must walk out the Kingdom of Heaven in our own lives and in the world around us.

Questions

1. Where are you taking Jesus, and what are you doing with Him?

2. Are you making choices out of love or out of religious obligation?

3. What is your primary motivation for being a Christian?

4. Are you ignorant of grace or offended by mercy?

Chapter 8

REJECTION IN COMMUNITY

My time in church and ministry communities was eye opening. I learned that church and ministry communities could become something not at all intended by the direct leadership of the movement. I was blessed enough to get to connect one-on-one with some well-known men and women in ministry over the years. I have gotten a glimpse into the hearts of some of these leaders of the "big ministries," and the thing that really shocked me was the vast difference between the leadership and the community. We as a community can also become what we perceive.

Oftentimes, I would think a leader was a certain way just from the initial community perspective, and I would base my personal identity on what I perceived to be signs of maturity and authority. Thus, I would think that to be taken seriously or to be viewed as a godly person, I must mimic the personhood of the leader I was idolizing. Unfortunately, that was the very thing I was doing, "idolizing," and it got me into a place of confusion. I would lead like that person, and I would say the things that person said, and even in the way they may have said them. You know you have idolized a leader in your life when others in the community start to tell you that you appear to be like this leader.

The issue of mimicry is not always a bad thing. On several occasions, the apostle Paul called on the early Church to be like him. There are leaders in our lives who should be living such good examples of Christ that we are inspired by the way they live. I hope that as a leader I exude a certain amount of Christ, and that others around me want some of that.

The problem comes when we are no longer following Jesus, but instead are looking to this person or to a corporate identity for approval. We become lost in our perspectives. It is not hard to be rejected in community when we have set up these leaders as gods.

We can at times deify a leader and treat him as if he is Christ. I know that on my own journey I found myself in a dark place where a leader became like Jesus to me. It took me years to allow the Holy Spirit to de-program me away from this state of thinking. Now, this was not entirely the leader's fault for my hardships from faulty foundations. The truth is, I allowed my perception to become distorted because I was fueled by the fear of man and not by my relationship with Jesus. I cared more about what this leader thought of my life than about what Jesus thought of me.

I opened myself to humiliating circumstances due to this
perversion of perspective. I couldn't stand against sin because

I was standing on a leader in my life that was not Jesus. You can't grow as a believer when you are not in line with who Jesus is. At this point of my life, I would have benefited so much more just by keeping Jesus as my identity.

It is important to keep in mind that you can create a dangerous situation for others as well as yourself when you live this way. Mine is not an uncommon story for those who have been involved in unhealthy churches or unhealthy ministry communities. This idolization also endangers the person you are deifying, because they then have to process this unquestioned level of loyalty and praise. We need to keep our identity with Jesus.

Questions

1. Do you know the difference between perception and truth?

2. What characteristics do you see in yourself that are similar to your pastor or those you hold in high regard?

3. Are you sure you know enough about who you are or who that leader is to start reproducing that perceived character within yourself? Is it a biblical attribute you are reproducing?

4. Are you creating a dangerous situation by deifying a leader in your life?

Chapter 9

EPHESIANS 2

The Messiah has made things up between us so that we're now together on this, both non-Jewish outsiders and Jewish insiders. He tore down the wall we used to keep each other at a distance. He repealed the law code that had become so clogged with fine print and footnotes that it hindered more than it helped. Then he started over. Instead of continuing with two groups of people separated by centuries of animosity and suspicion, he created a new kind of human being, a fresh start for everybody.

Christ brought us together through his death on the cross. The Cross got us to embrace, and that was the end of the hostility. Christ came and preached peace to you outsiders and peace to us insiders. He treated us as equals, and so made us equals. Through him we both share the same Spirit and have equal access to the Father (Ephesians 2:14-18 MSG).

We are a family now, and as believers, we don't have to have the same walls of competition and jealousy between us. All the hurts, rejection, suspicion, and disappointment that we have used to keep distance between us have been removed through Christ Jesus.

We have used lots of things to build up walls in the Church. We have used legalism, sin, religion, and pain to keep out of each other's lives. When we can label other Christians as sinners, it gives us the right to reject them. Once we reject someone through the law, we no longer have to extend love or grace to them.

Jesus came with a new covenant, demolishing the old law that had become so clogged with fine print and footnotes. The old law hindered more than it helped. Through the death of Jesus, He Himself created one new man! All that had separated us is now broken, if we choose to believe and are called according to His will.

Christ brought us together through His death on the cross. The sacrifice that Jesus paid got us to embrace, and that was the end of the hostility...we became family. Christ came and preached peace to us all, and this was the message of Christ: *"LOVE ONE ANOTHER."* (See John 15:12; Romans 12:10; Ephesians 4:2; 1 Thessalonians 3:12.)

Do you know that no one is more cared for than another by God? I am not more loved by God than you are. We are all looked at as equals. We should not show favoritism in the Kingdom. This also includes the way we treat ourselves, meaning don't consider yourself a "nobody" and everyone else a "somebody."

Do you realize that because of everything Jesus did, it is made true for us all? When Jesus treated us as equals, we became equals. When Jesus healed the sick, we all gained access to heal the sick. Literally, every action that Jesus did on earth was given to us as His heirs. Through Him we all share the same Spirit and have equal access to the Father. We all have the same Jesus living inside of us.

> *This kingdom of faith is now your home country. You're no longer strangers or outsiders. You belong here, with as much right to the name Christian as anyone. God is building a home. He's using us all—irrespective of how we got here—in what he is building. He used the apostles and prophets for the foundation. Now he's using you, fitting you in brick by brick, stone by stone, with Christ Jesus as the cornerstone that holds all the parts together. We see it taking shape day after day—a holy temple built by God, all of us built into it, a temple in which God is quite at home* (Ephesians 2:19-22 MSG).

So the major questions are, "Are we united in building a home for the Lord? Are we building a resting place?" Well, to answer those questions, we must ask another question. "Are YOU becoming a house for the Lord?" What we live internally and privately create the culture around us, and how we maintain our relationship with the Lord in private permeates the culture around us. What are we creating?

Questions

1. Do you truly believe that you are unique and have something to offer those around you?

2. Do you know the difference between not being able to be enough for others and knowing that you bring something special to your circle of family and friends?

3. I want you to ponder just some of the miracles that Jesus performed, and then think about the fact that when Jesus did that miracle, He had in His mind *you* doing it as well.

4. Did Jesus ever call us to do something we were not able to do or become something that we could never become?

Chapter 10

PERFORMANCE-BASED COMMUNITY

I have received so many emails over the past few months from people all over the world telling me their beautifully broken stories. You would be amazed at the amount of mishandling and spirit crushing that is going on in the Church on a global scale. I have heard stories of families getting ripped apart and people totally destroyed by well-meaning Christians. I am not addressing these stories to "punish" the church or church leadership, but instead to say we must be cautious when giving opinions over Scripture.

I hear story upon story of individuals who tried to keep up appearances and put their best feet forward only to be totally rejected and disheartened by their own failures. They are beautiful people who learned to dance and perform for their self-worth. It has been passed down since the fall to perform, posture, and hide your true self from God.

Most of these people learned to deify others in the Church, and you don't know what can come to life inside a person who is being deified. One of the biggest issues that can cause a situation to become unhealthy or unsafe is the development of legalism within the leader, church, ministry community, or the abused individual. When someone—either leader or victim—falls into the trap of legalism, it can make an already stressed situation completely fracture. When the leader becomes legalistic, it can very easily break the spirit of the individual who is being abused. When the person being abused gives himself or herself over to legalism, it puts them through a more intense level of being affected by the abuse. The issue of legalism is so important because it is a direct assault on the Blood of Christ.

> Legalism, in Christian theology, is a sometimes-pejorative term referring to an over-emphasis on law or codes of conduct, or legal ideas, usually implying an allegation of misguided rigor, pride, superficiality, the neglect of mercy, and ignorance of the grace of God or emphasizing the letter of law over the spirit. Legalism is alleged against any view that obedience to law, not faith in God's grace, is the pre-eminent principle of redemption.[1]

Even Paul in his day was constantly railing against this idea that there is another way to become righteous. In Paul's day there were other apostles who demanded of the people that they be circumcised to be in right standing with God. Paul was outraged at this demonic theology that was being pushed on the weak. Paul states, *"But even if we or an angel from heaven should preach to you a gospel contrary to the one we preached to you, let him be accursed"* (Gal. 1:8). This was a very big deal in the time of Paul, as it still is to this day among believers.

Oftentimes, people do not understand what legalism is. We think it's the angry person in the front row of the church in a suit or a person who is not outwardly as free as we are during worship. In actuality, it is a much greater issue than an outward appearance. It is in the heart that this demonic standard takes root and spreads into our teaching and into the culture. It is a weed that spreads and chokes out the beauty and authenticity of truth before God.

Legalism is the fuel behind performance-based Christianity. Legalism puts the main focus of your walk with the Lord under a specific religious list of dos and don'ts. Once we are able to look at other Christians as failures, we feel it gives us the right to reject them. It feels good to say, "Well, I would never do that," or "At least I'm not that bad." Honestly, as a leader, if you can't see yourself making some of the same mistakes as these "sinners," then my personal opinion is that you may not be ready to lead anyone.

Using this unhealthy way of relating to God, we gain approval through our ability to keep up our performance and the completion of our lists. We use these lists or personal taboos as a checklist of the things that keep us righteous. As long as we can count on these impersonal checklists, then we will never live in the freedom of an honest relationship. We will always relate to God on a performance-based relationship.

One dangerous aspect of performing for God is the fact that we can fail. Therefore if we measure our righteousness based on how well we "perform" and we fail in our performance, then it breeds a shame-based relationship with God. This has been a tragedy that has followed our forefathers since the fall.

On the other hand, when you set up your identity in Jesus, it seems like a direct attack to those who are not mature in their understanding of what it means to be made righteous. Living out of a relationship is uncomfortable to people at times because they are seeking approval and not relationship. It's sometimes easier to relate to a leader who is abusive when they demand things of you, then to a leader who leads through the power of relationship and love.

Why is it so much easier for some to pursue approval rather than relationship? I believe the reason we like to meet expectations rather than relationship is due to the naturally arising issue that we are fearful of not measuring up. If we can meet the list, then we measure up; but if we fail at a relationship, we have learned through the filters of life and experience that we have to reject or be rejected. If we meet the list of duties, then we cannot be rejected, but we will always be at an emotional distance from the relationship.

It is so nice to be proven before men. The idea of legalism works well on the front end mostly due to the fact that we get approved before our peers. The issue of self-esteem is vital in the church and yet so many go on through their life being hidden and refusing to address the fact that they are afraid of not being enough for others. If I can meet what others expect of me and appear powerful, strong, wise, or holy, then I never have to face the haunting thought deep down that I might not be enough for people.

Because we are fearful of relationship and intimacy, we like to examine others around us rather than looking inward at our own desperation. If I can tell you about the speck in your eye, then I do not have to look at the plank in my own (see Luke 6:41). We are at a critical point in the Western church where people are running around with big open wounds refusing treatment, all the while criticizing others for their own wounds. We have a bunch of people running about saying, "Act like you're not hurt, and don't let them see that you're weak." We have a church history of eating our wounded, when we are the very ones who are in desperate need of a doctor.

If you're a church leader, it would do you good to ask yourself, "Where am I drawing my strength and identity from? Is it from my congregation? From my interns? From my leadership team?" Leaders of ministries as well as those under their authority should be asking the same question of themselves, "Where is my identity from?"

Do you know what kind of pressure and drunken power can come from someone who is admonished and praised beyond what is healthy? This type of thing can be just as powerful as the depth of pain that comes from being rejected in community by this type of leader.

Within an unhealthy ministry community, there can be a level of reality to the statement, "Leaders are not like the misconceptions of their community." But there is also some great truth to the idea that a leader must realize that what privately motivates them may seep out into the community around them. As a leader you can only lead as far as you have repented and been transformed. When someone on your leadership team falls and no one knew anything about it, you must ask yourself "Why?" and "What in my own leadership contributed to this happening?" Even King David, when a harsh prophetic word was given to him, was given the opportunity to search his heart before God and ask, "Is there any truth in this, Lord?" (see 2 Sam. 12:1-15).

One of the dangerous aspects of rejection in community is this whole cycle of church cannibalism. Galatians 5:15 tells us to be careful not to backbite one another lest you devour each other. You see, in a ministry community, the idea that "knowledge equals power" takes on an ugly perversion. People in unhealthy community can think that the more they know about the private lives and struggles of others, the higher up on the ministry "corporate ladder" they are.

I remember observing this unhealthy behavior in many leadership meetings both within the ministry where I was a leader, as well as in other ministries I had relationship with. I would like to say that this was just a leadership issue in all of these circumstances, but unfortunately, it also tends to be a community issue. This happens because what you do as a leader permeates the culture you help create. That's why, whenever someone I am mentoring falls into a particular area of sin, I ask myself, *Lord, what part of my leadership, if any, contributed to this?*

We as an American culture—and really, most cultures— define our level of importance or value by what inside information we have about what's going on around us. "The more you know, the more valuable you are," is a basic business principle. Unfortunately, sometimes in our brokenness, we can take that into an unhealthy place. Many people in ministry communities would consider themselves more important based upon "private information."

Please don't misread what I am trying to get across in this section. The whole idea behind this chapter is to get us thinking outside of our broken cycles and to help us get back to our original identities. I am hoping that someone who is wounded and living in an unhealthy community will read this book and that they will start thinking for themselves. I am praying that Jesus will set right the people's perspectives. I am praying that leaders in ministry communities will read this book and that they will use it as a tool to train and equip their leaders as well as themselves on what healthy community looks like.

If we are going to look at the warning signs and negative aspects of an unhealthy ministry community, then we must also look at what the signs are of a *healthy* ministry community. In the previous section, I touched on what I observed that was unhealthy or abusive in ministries, but one thing I am adding now for the reader is this: I myself gave in to these unhealthy aspects of community. I found myself thriving on the knowledge of other people's personal lives. I was a religious freak show! The truth is that religious people *do* want to get into your personal life, so they can feel better about themselves and control you. I was the chief sinner in this regard.

One of the beauties of revelation from God is that it sets you free. Once you have that moment when your mind connects with the truth and you are awakened, beauty arises in your heart and you are given a chance to get free! What a wonderful feeling it was to know that I didn't have to live that way anymore. Learning that Jesus was my identity and that I didn't need to perform or prove myself to anyone was one of the best moments in my life!

I am still in the process of accepting the freedom of truth. This is not just a one-time thing where you get the revelation and then, all of a sudden, that's it, and you never need to dwell on it again. Once the revelation comes, you need it over and over again. It's a lot like forgiveness, in that you must progressively forgive and forget. You must continually speak the truth of the revelation you received in order to really grab hold of it.

Fear is the primary motivation behind performance-based relationships. Man's fear is a debilitating disease that has been breaking our hearts for centuries. The Lord wants us to look to Him as our point of confidence. We are to live in the fullness of our personalities and emotions in our relationship with the Father.

Fear and guilt are two very powerful components of spiritual abuse. These two forces can cause people to live their lives striving to get the approval of their religious leaders and fellow group members—many times to the detriment of themselves and their family members.

Being Aware of Spiritual Abuse

Fear is what enables us to lean toward spiritual abuse to begin with. While we are in a spiritually abusive relationship, we have the abuser constantly implying (or even flat out telling us) that if we don't meet their level of expectations, then satan will take over our finances, relationships, or family. We are taught that if we leave "the covering" of the abusive leader, satan will destroy us. This is how we get locked into a spiritually abusive relationship.

The entire time we are in these groups, we are being continually programmed with fear. This is why we find ourselves bound with fear, panic attacks, anxiety, or even depression after leaving these abusive groups. It is also not uncommon for people who are being abused to feel those same feelings when they are alone; thus, the thought of expulsion is paralyzing. It can take years to get deprogrammed from this fear—but we can be *reprogrammed* to have the mind of Christ, by educating ourselves, by renewing our minds, and by washing in the water of the Word.

When I was walking through a particularly hard season where I was so afraid and broken, I found myself in a weird place both mentally and emotionally. I knew that I had sinned and thus was at fault for my current state of pain, but at the same time, there was this giant red flashing light saying, "Warning… Warning…." The cause for concern was due to how I was being handled or "restored."

I was so scared to fail and be cast out into "the world" with no "covering" that I had several anxiety attacks over a two-year period. I viewed the world as if it were satan's playground, and I feared that I would be vulnerable to his attacks after I left my former ministry's "authority and protection."

I viewed the outside church as a poor and weak environment. It was spoken of as being deluded and on the edge of apathy. The church outside of our ministry didn't have the level of revelation that we had, which meant they were fooled by the "doctrine of demons." On several occasions, I heard leaders in classes make degrading statements about the frailty and poor character of other Christian denominations or movements. Unfortunately, I wholeheartedly bought into this way of thinking. It produced such elitism in almost everyone I knew in the ministry as well as in myself. One of the most valuable lessons I learned from this process was that true biblical, Spirit-led revelation should produce a *greater love* for those around you—not give you a reason to reject them, label them as sinners, or give you some sort of legal right to become elitist.

I think we need to be careful about all the sharp, cutting, or strong things we say in the name of truth. If our "enlightenment" is not producing love, then it's not truth. We should never sacrifice the sincerity and kindness of God for the sake of building a strong reputation as a cutting edge speaker or movement. I don't think we should ever want to be considered powerful over compassionate. The best kind of truth is a Christ-centered truth, and the truth of Christ will never remove any believer's dignity.

How do we deal with this performance-based lifestyle? For one, we need to accept the fact that we cannot attain perfection, religious or otherwise. Then we need to let everyone else in our lives know this too—especially those with whom we have had performance-based relationships in the past. We need to constantly remind ourselves that it's OK to fail, OK to make mistakes, OK to let others down—it's all part of being human. We have to counter the message that told us, "You are only worth something if you perform properly." It can be very stressful and frustrating when our worth as a person is based on our religious performance. Healthy relationships allow us to be human, and they accept our whole package as a person—strengths and weaknesses included—without trying to make us measure up to another's standards. We need to embrace the idea of the Church being a safe place to fail.

Questions

1. Do you feel that your church and/or ministry is a safe place to fail?

2. If you are a ministry leader or pastor, could you put yourself in the shoes of the person you are restoring? Could you see yourself making those same mistakes?

3. Are you going strong for God—personally as well as in community—based on being approved and loved or earning approval and love?

Endnote

1. Wikipedia contributors, "Legalism (theology)," *Wikipedia, The Free Encyclopedia,* http://en.wikipedia.org/w/index.php?title=Legalism_(theology)&oldid=339286422 (accessed January 27, 2010).

Chapter 11

SPIRITUAL ABUSE

Spiritual abuse occurs when a person in religious authority misleads, manipulates, or overpowers the will of another person in the name of God, the Church, or in the unattainable mystery of any spiritual concept. When we use the term "spiritual abuse," it often is in reference to an individual who is using spiritual or religious rank to take advantage of the victim's spirituality by putting the victim in a state of unquestioning obedience to an abusive authority or abusive mindset.

Spiritual abuse can include any of the following:[1]

- Psychological and emotional abuse

- Any act, spoken or acted out, that demeans, humiliates, or shames the natural worth and dignity of a person as a human being

- Submission to spiritual authority without any right to disagree (through the use of intimidation)

- Unreasonable control of a person's basic right to make a choice on spiritual matters

- False accusation and repeated criticism by negatively labeling a person as disobedient, rebellious, lacking faith, demonized, apostate, enemy of the church or God

- Isolation or separation from family and friends due to religious affiliation

- Physical abuse that includes physical injury, deprivation of sustenance, and sexual abuse

- Exclusivity; dismissal of an outsider's criticism and labeling an outsider as of the devil or not enlightened

- Withholding information and giving of information only to a selected few

- Conformity to a dangerous or unnatural religious view and practice

- Hostility that includes shunning (relational aggression, parental alienation) and persecution

The terms *church abuse* and *religious abuse* are often associated with spiritual abuse. Church abuse is a distinctive label for the abusive practices done inside a church. Religious abuse is used interchangeably with church abuse, but it is more of an abuse related to deviation from truth in an organized belief system and communal practice than to personal conviction or personal affiliation.

Researchers conceptualize a set of discernible characteristics of spiritual abuse. Dr. Ronald Enroth, in his book *Churches That Abuse*, identifies five categories:[2]

1. **Authority and Power**—abusive groups misuse and distort the concept of spiritual authority. Abuse arises when leaders of a group arrogate to themselves power and authority that lack the dynamics of open accountability and the capacity to question or challenge decisions made by leaders. The shift entails moving from general respect for an office bearer to one where members loyally submit without any right to dissent.

2. **Manipulation and Control**—abusive groups are characterized by social dynamics where fear, guilt, and threats are routinely used to produce unquestioning obedience, group conformity, and stringent tests of loyalty to the leaders are demonstrated before the group. Biblical concepts of the leader-disciple relationship tend to develop into a hierarchy where the leader's decisions control and usurp

the disciple's right or capacity to make choices on spiritual matters or even in daily routines of what form of employment, form of diet, and clothing are permitted.

Let me say this as a side note on manipulation. I have had many people ask me what a false prophet is. I have had people tell me their own stories of moving out in immaturity in their prophetic gifting and being labeled as a false prophet. Being immature or even being wrong does not make you a false prophet, but using prophecy to manipulate others, I believe, *does* meet the definition of false prophet.

3. **Elitism and Persecution**—abusive groups depict themselves as unique and have a strong organizational tendency to be separate from other bodies and institutions. The social dynamism of the group involves being independent or separate, with diminishing possibilities for internal correction and reflection. Outside criticism and evaluation is dismissed as the disruptive efforts of evil people seeking to hinder or thwart.

4. **Lifestyle and Experience**—abusive groups foster rigidity in behavior and in belief that requires unswerving conformity to the group's ideals and social mores.

5. **Dissent and Discipline**—abusive groups tend to suppress any kind of internal challenges and

dissent concerning decisions made by leaders. Acts of discipline may involve emotional and physical humiliation, physical violence or deprivation, acute and intense acts of punishment for dissent and disobedience.

Agnes and John Lawless in *Drift into Deception: The Eight Characteristics of Abusive Christianity* find that there are eight major characteristics of spiritual abuse within a ministry community or church setting:[3] This is from personal study on and college textbooks

1. Pride

2. Anger and Intimidation

3. Greed and Fraud

4. Immorality

5. Enslaving Authoritarian Structure

6. Exclusivity

7. Demanding Loyalty and Honor

8. New Revelation that produces Elitism.

Although some of these points form aspects of a strong and healthy society (e.g. respect for proper authority, loyalty, and honor), the basis of spiritual abuse is when these characteristics are overstretched to achieve a desired goal that is neither supported by spiritual reality nor by the human conscience.

The following comments about how to recognize spiritual abuse are excerpted from *Twisted Scriptures* by Mary Alice Chrnalogar:[4]

If you have experienced any of these conditions in your church, it may indicate a misuse of Scripture and/or may represent the presence of abuse and excessive control:

- The church sees itself as "more committed" to Jesus than those not in the church.

- Church members are rebuked for actions that aren't really sinful but which merely differ from the leaders' opinions.

- The leader uses verses such as "Touch not my anointed" to imply we can't criticize leaders without being critical of God.

- The group teaches people to obey even when it doesn't feel right.

- The leader teaches that the Bible says to stay away from those who have "fallen away."

- The leader teaches that "following Christ" means giving up all personal wishes, desires, and goals.

- The leaders [supposedly] can hear God and know God's will better than you can.

- The gray and open areas of your life become narrowed, and absolute rights and wrongs are made very clear.

- Your group or church believes it has the only valid baptism.

- You become extremely irritated when someone criticizes your group or leaders.

- Those who disagree with, or openly challenge, leaders are "causing divisions."

- You choose not to associate with people who cause you to question your beliefs.

- To a great degree, you are disconnected from Christians outside your group and from those who have left it.

- You frequently feel you are not being open when you don't confess or share all aspects of your personal life.

- You are told that being secretive is a sin.

- Other churches simply "do it wrong."

- You do not wish to include unbelievers in your social life.

- [When you are dating,] your leader exerts control that is as bad as or worse than a domineering parent.

- Your leader talks about being "unequally yoked" when discussing potential mates not in your group.

- You avoid reading books that might challenge your beliefs.

- You are told examples of bad things that happened to people who left your group.

- You feel guilty when you make your own decisions that go against the approval of your leader (in dealing with non-moral issues).

- Since your involvement in the group, you have little time for your family and have missed important personal commitments in order to attend group meetings or church activities.

- The leaders publicly rebuke or discipline members for matters that are not necessary to expose to the whole church.

- The leaders repeatedly and emphatically request money (and stress that a lack of financial giving is an indication of an unhealthy spiritual life).

Part of the reason that I am providing so much information about spiritual abuse is due to the lack of education on this specific topic in church and ministry communities. So many Christians just keep moving forward, not knowing they are being abused. They think that it's normal to live this way. Unhealthy community relations get passed down from generation to generation without anyone finding out what the Bible says about the issues of spiritual abuse or healthy community.

When I was going through my own counseling with a friend in Dallas, Texas, I made the comment, "I wish I had my old personality." When that statement came out of my mouth, it was as if a light from Heaven had penetrated my heart, and all of a sudden I understood that I had lost a perspective of my original personality while I was in an unhealthy ministry community. I had replaced my original personality with the idealized image of the leader in my life and of the ministry community I was living in.

I thought to myself, *God, how did this happen? How did I lose myself in this community?* I had taken every beautiful aspect of my personality and wound up replacing it with the larger collective. I remember visiting home from time to time, and old friends that I grew up with as well as family members were thrown for a loop due to the recent change in my personality. I was no longer the funny, curly-haired, fun-loving guy they remembered. I had lost what made me unique, which is a crime against God and the person who God created me to be.

I began a journey with these questions: How do I get back to that place? How do I remove the persona that I took on as my personality, and embrace the "me" underneath the false self? I have spent the last three years on this journey of traveling back in time with the healing power of the Holy Spirit to find my true self. The Lord has walked me through a deep healing process as it pertains to being deprogrammed and retrieving my original self. I have defrosted and started to bloom again.

Many hurting Christians out there need to go on this kind of journey. There are so many wounded, beautiful, broken individuals in the Body of Christ who need to be set free and awakened. The community should always support the original personality and identity of all individuals in order to be truly effective in producing healthy believers.

Any ministry or church that we are involved in should help provide an education system that helps our character grow, but at the same time helps us keep our original personalities. We should be called to progressively grow in godly character as we walk out our faith, while keeping our original identity.

With spiritual abuse it is often very difficult to find any evidence of abuse. Those being abused often fail to recognize what is happening due to peer pressure or the use of guilt feelings in relation to obedience toward the leaders of a church/group/fellowship or cult, etc., which can be masked as obedience toward God. This again is a prime example of the need for healthy church and ministry communities.

As cited by Ronald Enroth in *Churches That Abuse,* control-oriented leadership is at the core of all such religious groups. Additionally, as interpersonal relations in "spiritual government" environments are considered above the "worldly" need of documented accountability, rarely are conversations or spiritually abusive situations recorded for historical reference and archiving. The usual attitude of delegated or "deputy" authority in a spiritually abusive environment is such that the abusive one(s) consider their speaking to be absolute—fully expecting immediate submission and unquestioned obedience. Any reticence or hesitation is interpreted as hidden rebellion against the "deputy."

Generally, the attitude exists that if anyone has concerns or uneasy feelings about spiritually abusive activities or puts into question the behaviors or actions of a leader, they are accused of not being in submission to authority and could even suffer from extreme character assassination (both privately and publicly) in order to diminish the effect of any desire of clarification that could liberate themselves and/or others from a spiritually abusive person/situation. YES!

Leaving an abusive church or ministry community is normally a process that can take a few months or even years. Children in a spiritually abusive situation may be unable to leave. For those who are able to leave, it can be extremely difficult and painful emotionally, socially, and psychologically. In certain cases, an individual who feels spiritually abused will have to leave immediate family and friends behind and even suffer rejection by them. It is important for such a person to get help, such as counseling from "outsiders," who are not part of the spiritually abusive group. They also need support from new peers because of the effects of spiritual abuse that will continue to affect them. This abused individual needs to learn a new way of looking at the world so this process literally turns their world upside down; it would be impossible to walk this path alone.[5]

We learn that most abused individuals will have a very hard time trusting anyone around them, especially Christians and the Church. A healthy team of well-balanced believers are needed to provide a support system, but survivors will have difficulty gravitating toward others and for sure they will have trouble breaking free from their dependency patterns. Communal social support through the ministry of hospitality is vital for those who have escaped such an abusive environment. You can show this hospitality simply by being an honest friend to these individuals. You can offer to take them to the movies, to dinner, or out for coffee. Much trust can be built in a relationship that is normal and honest. This is not the time for intensity or to treat the abused individual as a project that needs to be worked on. Make sure when you are befriending an individual who has been victimized in this way that you are refraining from a conversation about church or religious issues unless directed by the individual or the gentleness of the Holy Spirit.

It is common for those who have been spiritually abused or who have gone through deep rejection to experience a strong level of emotion. The longer the individual had to stay in the community and endure abuse without an outlet for emotions, the longer it will take for them to experience the full range of emotions about it. Just think of it like this: The length of time you experienced the abuse will more than likely be the same amount of time it takes to get back to your true self.

When walking someone through the healing process, you will not want to rely on some deep theology, but instead let it simply be about freely expressed emotion. Fear, guilt, anger, grief, rage, sorrow—all must be felt and expressed in their time. An over-spiritualizing of emotions may have been present in the dysfunctional ministry community.

We must become a safe and stable place for broken individuals, a place to be calm without expectations of performance. We must deny the desire to lord over any individual or become too involved in private lives. These individuals that are on the path to healing were given a demonic doctrine not to trust others or their teaching, so it is imperative that we do not press the individual for a premature level of trust. We must remember that it is about the person who is going through the healing; it is not about us.

Oftentimes, in Western culture, we have an inaccurate view of what level of intimacy we are at with other individuals, thus feeling rejected when we are not fully trusted 100 percent right off the bat. Don't push the individual. Don't push the recovery process. Respect their boundaries, and remember the phrase: "It's about them and not about you."

So much healing can come from us just listening to others and not just waiting for our chance to talk. People across the board who have been wounded by rejection or spiritual abuse need to tell their stories to get a level of freedom and interpersonal intimacy with others. This is part of the journey I went on myself to find out who I was again. I told my story so I would remember who I was. I also needed to tell my story so I could own all aspects of it. I wanted to be able to say, "Yes, there were things that were done wrong to me and there were things that I did wrong as well." I needed to get to a place where I could trust God with what had been done to me, as well as trust God with what I had done.

People who have lost their identities need to be validated by others who believe them. It's important to talk these things out so they can use the truth to remove the wrong perspectives and teachings from their mindset of the past and also discern abuse in the future. Most individuals who were abused in these unhealthy communities were taught not to talk at all about the group or the leaders, so our listening when they choose to open up is a vital and powerful thing.

Encourage the individuals who have been mishandled and abused to tell their stories. Listen. Empathize. Offer words that may give language to what the individual is feeling. The abused individual may not even fully be aware of what they are feeling themselves. Remember that it is not about you directly, so try not to bring the focus back on you, but instead offer comments and supportive statements. Keep confidentiality. Be trustworthy.

Survivors typically do not know who they are anymore. They have lost themselves in the church or cult. Most abusive ministries have a process of replacing the true identity of the abused individual with the corporate identity. This is often the time that individuals will even go as far as taking on another identity. The unhealthy ministry or church will sometimes unknowingly walk its members through a process that goes something like this: They will drastically change the lifestyle of the person being victimized. Oftentimes they will bog down the individual with chores and tasks to keep them busy and tired. Couple this "busy" lifestyle with sleep deprivation, and you have individuals who are living in a shaken and moldable mental state.

This is what psychologists refer to as the "Freezing Process." Usually during this process, the individuals receiving the abuse are asked to make choices they would never consider making previously. They are asked to have limited contact with the "outside," including members of their family and/or loved ones. The individuals are deemed as too weak to carry on these relationships. Often the relationships are looked at as ungodly because of conflicting views of the ministry.

In the search for their true identity, those who have been abused need to know that they have worth as human beings. When talking with these beautifully broken victims, count them as equal to yourself—not less just because they are needy or desperate. It is vital to let the people who are victimized by these situations know that they are not perfect and that performance-based godliness is not a biblical reality. Accept them as they are and offer hospitality as well as encouragement. God will use you in a powerful and bold way in your relationship with others who have been spiritually abused by using you to help build confidence.

It is very important for those who have been abused to feel like they have a choice in all general aspects of their lives. We must learn to offer choices to the individual. Let them know that they don't have to be perfect, and make sure they feel the freedom to have strengths and weaknesses.

They need to know that they are not being influenced by the devil or demonized. We need to encourage the empowerment of choice, so they know they can move forward into a new realm of freedom. In pursuing freedom, we want to make sure that people don't try to make decisions for those who were already given no choice.

One powerful tool is to be truthful about yourself and the shortcomings of your church. No church is perfect and no person will be perfect until Jesus returns. It is good to admit that you are a normal human being capable of mistakes, and it is a good thing to admit your own inability to have all the answers. Speaking the truth of who you are or who your church is will not destroy any hope for their relationship with God. Remember, it is the Holy Spirit's job to draw them to

Him. Your freedom in admitting that you are not perfect and that neither you nor your church have all the answers may help those who struggle to learn that struggling is OK, that not having all the answers is OK as well. Much freedom can come from people saying, "OK, God, I don't know." It may be the very thing that helps those who are coming out of spiritually abusive situations to come to terms with the fact that it's OK to study.

One of the best grounds that we can gain is a right and true perspective of God. It is critical that survivors know that God is not the group. Leaving the ministry or church is not equivalent to leaving the faith or abandoning God. One thing we want to make sure of is that people know that no ministry or church has an exclusive truth. No ministry or church should gain an elitist attitude based on any form of revelation. True Holy Spirit-led revelation should only produce intimacy and humility.

Even though this section is largely about how to help and assist those who are coming out of spiritually abusive situations, we always want to remember that our friendship to the person must be sincere. They are not a project. As much as we struggle with wanting to fix everything and have an answer for every situation, it is good that we don't try to fix them. It is good for the individual to see that we don't always have the answer, because they were in a situation where the one lording over them always did have an answer. Let them know you speak for yourself. This is not necessarily the time to speak prophetically on behalf of the Lord. There are several ways to minister prophetically to a broken individual without pushing them into a corner.

As I stated earlier, we must acknowledge and trust God with what was done by the ministry or church leaders. We must encourage the abused individual to admit that the ministry or church leader is hurting and deceiving people. Be gentle and try not to be over-spiritual as you give feedback on what was hurtful and wrong in the group. Remember that the person who has left or who is being excommunicated may have left some very dear friends, family, and loved ones behind.

Some of you may be asking, "When do we start bringing the truth of the Bible into this relationship?" Do not be in a religious rush to start stuffing the Bible down their throats. The truth is that most of these individuals will not attend church or read the Bible for quite some time. This is normal. It is actually by the kindness of God that He will gently and lovingly bring an abused individual back into the church and Bible reading when the individual is ready.

As these victims of spiritual abuse lost their own identity in the community, they also lost the true identity and nature of God. Those who have been programmed in this way will need to, in a sense, start over with the process of faith. Those individuals will need to have the basics of the faith explained to them once again. They will need to have grace explained in depth and to examine God's attributes carefully.

When someone is coming out of an abusive church or ministry, it can be a long process that will involve realizing many areas of their belief system have been wrong due to the twisting of Scripture or theology by a ministry or church. Individuals will need to be progressively reminded of the true attributes of God and the principle of grace. Be genuine.

Be personal. Explain how Scripture helps you to understand God's attributes. Open up and let the individual know how you got to where you are with your perspective of God. Again, only go down this road when you perceive the individual is ready for this type of conversation. To become reconciled to God requires reconciliation with God's people. Many who begin to trust God again have much more difficulty trusting people in any church. It helps to confront the truth about God's people.

When someone is wounded and on the journey of healing from spiritual abuse, we can best serve them through honesty, loving them by helping them to recognize the distorted thinking that accompanies these tragic histories. The Holy Spirit will bring alignment to their perspectives of God, church, community, and basic interpersonal relationships. This is a good time to use the gentleness and authority of Scripture coupled with the revelatory power of the Holy Spirit to confront the deception created by the abusive group. Much positive progress can come from this type of relationship; it can bring much comfort and peace to those who are broken.

Almost everyone who comes through this type of spiritual abuse will need help working through their history, memories, and feelings triggered by certain situations. Church community and the Bible were perverted, deifying the leaders of the previous ministry or church. The Bible brings life and clarity. *God is not the author of confusion but of peace*" (1 Cor. 14:33 NKJV).

Challenge every concept, all usage of jargon and Bible language, for clarification of what it means to them.   137

Deprogramming those who have been abused takes time, dedication, patience, love, and diligent work. It helps us to not make assumptions about where the abused individual is currently in the areas of spirituality, emotional well-being, or in their understanding of the Bible and the character of God. Respect their spiritual boundaries while embracing the spirit of truth.

Let me say that these steps are a tool to be used under the umbrella of friendship, and some of these steps of healing should only be administered through a trained counselor who has experience with this part of spiritual abuse recovery.

As I said earlier, it may take months or even years for victims of spiritual abuse to get back into a church setting. These brave ones who have been mishandled by ministries, individuals, or churches may need time before returning to the Church, and that's OK. People who have been spiritually abused need help working through the memories and emotions triggered by going to church. Remember to point them to the truth in the Word and the true character of God Himself.

Again, only do this when the spiritually abused individual is ready to start the journey of healing their past. Those who have been abused will find it hard, but they need to know that God is not always tied to the actions of His people. In fact, some abusive ministry leaders and Christians never meant to hurt, control, or abuse people. However, the cycle of spiritual abuse can be passed down from leadership over the years simply because of lack of education and spiritual maturity. There are some people who truly meant well, and some who with full knowledge became deceptive to control their people or community.

Truth is a powerful tool for survivors. It is good for the victims of spiritual abuse to see that Christians are individuals and cannot all be lumped into the same compartment as those who hurt them. But that is the real gamble here. When it comes to healing, there is almost always risk involved. Christians and ministry communities were never meant to be put on pedestals, but to share revelation, encouragement, love, and strength with the greater Body of Christ and the world.

Questions

1. Do you feel that it is safe to admit your own weaknesses to yourself or in front of your leadership team?

2. Do you feel that it is safe to admit your pastor or ministry leader's weaknesses to yourself or others?

3. How many of the points from this chapter on spiritual abuse do you feel sound very familiar to you?

4. How can you use this chapter to provide a safe church or ministry community?

Endnotes

1.   Wikipedia contributors, "Spiritual abuse," *Wikipedia, The Free Encyclopedia,* http://en.wikipedia.org/w/index.php?title=Spiritual_abuse&oldid=338442411; accessed 1/27/10.

2.   Ronald Enroth, *Churches That Abuse* (Grand Rapids, MI: Zondervan, 1993).

3.   Agnes C. Lawless and John W. Lawless, *The Drift into Deception: The Eight Characteristics of Abusive Christianity* (Grand Rapids, MI: Kregel Publications, 1995).

4.   Mary Alice Chrnalogar, *Twisted Scriptures* (Grand Rapids, MI: Zondervan 2000).

5.   See note 1 above.

THE SCIENCE OF FORGIVENESS

Prior to the 1980s, forgiveness was a practice primarily left to the community of faith. Although there is presently no consensual psychological definition of forgiveness in the research literature, a consensus has emerged that forgiveness is a process and a number of models describing the process of forgiveness have been published, including one from a radical behavioral perspective.

Dr. Robert Enright from the University of Wisconsin–Madison founded the International Forgiveness Institute and is considered the initiator of secular forgiveness studies. He developed a 20-Step Process Model of Forgiveness. Recent work has focused on what kind of person is more likely to be forgiving. A longitudinal study showed that people who were generally more neurotic, angry, and hostile in life were less likely to forgive another person even after a long time had passed. Specifically, these people were more likely to still avoid their transgressor and want to enact revenge upon them four and a half years after the transgression.

Studies show that people who forgive are happier and healthier than those who hold resentments. The first study to look at how forgiveness improves physical health discovered that when people think about forgiving an offender, it leads to improved functioning in their cardiovascular and nervous systems. Another study at the University of Wisconsin found that the more forgiving people were, the less they suffered from a wide range of illnesses. The less forgiving people reported a greater number of health problems.

The research of Dr. Fred Luskin of Stanford University shows that forgiveness can be learned. In three separate studies, including one with Catholics and Protestants from Northern Ireland whose family members were murdered in the political violence, Dr. Luskin found that people who are taught how to forgive become less angry, feel less hurt, are more optimistic, become more forgiving in a variety of situations, and become more compassionate and self-confident. His studies show a reduction in experience of stress, physical manifestations of stress, and an increase in vitality.

One study has shown that the positive benefit of forgiveness is similar whether it was based upon religious or secular counseling as opposed to a control group that received no forgiveness counseling.[1]

Dr. Robert Enright gives a basic outline[2] to what Forgiveness means in a secular context:

1. What it is:

Moral

- It is a response to an injustice (a moral wrong). It is a turning to the "good" in the face of this wrongdoing.

Goodwill

- Merciful restraint from pursuing resentment or revenge. Generosity or offering good things such as: attention, time, and remembrances on holidays.

- Moral Love or contributing to the betterment of the other.

Paradoxical

- It is the foregoing of resentment or revenge when the wrongdoer's actions deserve it and giving the gifts of mercy, generosity, and love when the wrongdoer does not deserve them.

- As we give the gift of forgiveness we ourselves are healed.

Beyond duty

- A freely chosen gift (rather than a grim obligation).

- The overcoming of wrongdoing with good.

2. *What it is not:*

Forgetting/Denial

- Time passing/ignoring the effects of the wrongdoing.

Condoning

- Nothing that bad happened. It was only this one time. It won't happen again.

Excusing

- The person did this because…it wasn't really their responsibility.

Condemning

- She/he deserves to know they have wronged me.

"Forgiving"

- With a sense of moral superiority.

Seeking Justice or Compensation

- Forgiveness is not a quid pro quo deal—it doesn't demand compensation first.

3. Important Distinction:

Forgiveness

- One person's moral response to another's injustice

Reconciliation

- Two parties coming together in mutual respect for the restoration of a relationship.

The reason I felt it necessary to discuss the secular scientific aspect of forgiveness is due to the indisputable evidence that comes biologically from the act of forgiving. God put it in our DNA that when we choose to forgive, our body naturally comes into peace and health. We gain a physical and mental well-being. I think oftentimes in Christian culture we deny the truth of science out of fear of God being dismissed from the equation. But if you look at this in the light of God's wisdom and kindness, I find that science can give God a giant paintbrush, so to speak.

When you study physics or space under the filter of God's handiwork, your heart can come alive! The intricacies that God has created within us are awe-inspiring. Connecting that it is God's work is the critical point that I believe most scientists don't make and even many Christians are not willing to explore.

It is impossible to reap the full benefits of forgiveness without the God factor. Yes, your body may feel at peace, but it is not the fullness of what God had intended. You can settle for less and forgive without God and still feel the biological benefits because God doesn't take back His gifts, but I tell you if you forgive out of a choice based on faith and God, then you will have greater fruit than just a biological reaction. You will have a maturity and strength that comes to your very inner being!

Questions

1. Do you routinely practice genuine forgiveness? Or only occasionally?

2. Are there people waiting for you to forgive them? What is holding you back?

3. Do you believe, or have you had a personal experience, that unforgiveness can cause physical, emotional, and mental distress?

4. Do people have the ability to fully forgive without the help of God's mercy and grace? Why or why not?

Endnotes

1.   Wikipedia contributors, "Forgiveness," *Wikipedia, The Free Encyclopedia,* http://en.wikipedia.org/w/index.php?title=Forgiveness&oldid=339120871(accessed January 27, 2010).

2.   Covenant House Ministries, "Client Handbook: Addictions Recovery Program," http://www.scribd.com/doc/22300358/Covenant-House- Ministries-Client-Handbook-Addictions-Recovery-Program (accessed January 27, 2010).

Chapter 13

BITTERNESS VERSUS
FORGIVENESS

At the beginning of this book, we asked, *Where do we take the pain?* We are now faced with the closet that we have stuffed our old skeletons into. I once had a prophetic encounter when I was driving through the neighborhood where I grew up. While driving down those narrow broken roads, I started to see into the supernatural. I was visiting my hometown because I was on a journey where I was trying to find myself. I was in a desperate place where I learned that forward progression is sometimes the best place to live.

While I was on this drive, I saw skeletons on the front porches of all the houses in my old neighborhood. The Holy Spirit spoke the phrase to me, "They've opened their closets and hung their skeletons on their front porches like ornaments, hoping that their bones would blend right in." I opened a dialogue with the Holy Spirit about this vision and learned through this that many people openly live with hidden bitterness. I suppose it's a bit of a thought twister that people live out in the open with hidden bitterness, but I don't think it's such a stretch for us as godly inspired creations to connect with the subtleties under the surface. It is not uncommon for Holy Spirit-filled people to become sensitive to the system of the supernatural and see a little deeper.

What do we decide to do with our pain from the wounds that are sure to come in this life? It seems that even the average person who is not fully illuminated with the revelation of God is aware of the pains caused by life and the need or hunger for wholeness. Every person on this earth who is capable of feeling cannot deny the ache that is within them to feel love and through that love be made whole. It is wired into our very DNA to connect with love and all the benefits that love brings to our mind, body, and soul.

In my life I have seen incredibly dark people do very dark things to each other. But even in those people whose lives are ruled by the darkness of this world, I could begin to see the winter frost lose its grip. I have seen the ground thaw in the lives of people whose stories would make it difficult for you to finish your meal. I have seen people whom I was literally afraid of become suddenly vulnerable. I have seen the most broken people come forth and drop their false image and for a brief moment let their true self come to the surface gasping for air and asking for some kind of help.

The truth is that no one wants to hold onto bitterness. No one in the very core of their being wants to have that kind of pain, stress, or sickness bottled up inside them. Some people have suppressed their desire to be free from bitterness. I have dealt many times with bitterness and wanting to hold onto pain, so much so that this desire to have healing comes out through my dream life. I have spoken with many people who are holding onto their pain and thus producing bitterness.

I had one close friend tell me that the only time he made amends with the person who wounded him was in his dreams. He said he would wake up in the morning and feel such a deep hollow feeling in his stomach. He would be so close to walking out that forgiveness and moving on into wholeness and then, *wham*, he would wake-up back at square one.

When people act toward us in a way that is unappreciative or ungrateful, their behavior makes it that much more difficult to walk in forgiveness. For instance, you loved someone without being loved. You sacrificed to help a friend in need, only to be criticized or taken for granted. The person you went out of your way to help shows nothing but ingratitude and selfishness in return. Your good intentions are misinterpreted, and your good deeds are misconstrued as being selfishly motivated. In disbelief, you exclaim, "How can they be that way, after all I've done for them? So that's what I get for being so big-hearted?" Do we ever forgive that ungrateful person? We smile at them, wave a greeting from a distance, but we determine to "never do anything for them again."

We find it nearly impossible to forgive anyone who deceives us. We are most anxious to be forgiven for our own lies and failures, but nothing infuriates us more than to discover someone has lied to us. It is considered a breach of trust. We so quickly lose respect for that person. If we do 151 forgive, it is always qualified with, "I'll forgive you this time, but if you ever lie to me again, you've had it with me."

We really have trouble forgiving those who tell us we're wrong. Convinced we have a good reason for everything we do, we find it nearly impossible to forgive the person who suggests we have made a mistake. Rather than take an honest look at what that person is saying to us, we go into a long, involved explanation, justifying our actions. The closer our critics are to the truth, the less likely we are to forgive them for bringing it to our attention.

Some people can find a false strength or identity in bitterness. Some can take that pain, anger, or hurt and turn it around into a defense mechanism. This provides a false sense of one's strength and identity, but it is a weak foundation that will eventually come falling down. There are some truths that are as old as time and will never change no matter the pain or distress that someone might feel. I suppose it seems at first more comforting to stand on your own strength than to trust God. It is not uncommon for those who are dealing with bitterness to walk in a controlling spirit.

It is very hard to trust God with what someone has done to us or what we have done to someone else. This is where control meets letting go. Do we trust God? Do we trust that God will fully walk out our situation the best way possible? Or do we desire to take control and snatch the situation back out of His hands for fear that God might mishandle it?

We in our misunderstanding of the character and nature of God think that He doesn't know what is important to us or that somehow God can't relate to the level of pain we feel from what was done to us or others. The truth is that our pain and bitterness can very quickly become idolatry. If we lift anything above Christ, it becomes idolatry. Yes, even our pain…especially our pain.

We must not limit the all-encompassing and eternal power of God to renew and heal our situations. You have to know that His ways are not our ways and His thoughts are not our thoughts. We struggle with the unseen aspect of the Godhead in our lives, yet we must surrender ourselves to the perfect leadership of the Trinity.

I daresay that when our lives are impacted with rejection, abuse, loss, or general tragedy, we find our true faith or lack thereof. I think true faith and true Christianity come from the survival of tragedy. It is from the place of testing that we show our true theology. I would even make the bold statement that the truest faith is forged in the fires of trial. Some of the strongest Christians I have met have been pushed to the edge of Christianity onto the border of atheism.

Peter says to make your faith your own (see 2 Peter 1:3). That to me means to own your faith. We need a faith that is worn like leather and as pure as gold. So much of this walk with the Lord is personal. King David took things very personally on behalf of the Lord and in the name of his faith. King David was a man after God's own heart, and I believe it was due to his intimacy with the Lord, which in turn produced a personal covenant relationship for David. David survived some pretty tragic things, and I think it's safe to say that King David was pushed to the edge and made his faith his own. David had a choice at many points of his life to choose bitterness over forgiveness, but David did everything the Lord required of him.

How do we forgive?

Many of us, at the very core of our being, know that it is good to forgive. We know that we can benefit and move on in life through the power of forgiveness. We can choose to forgive others as well as forgive ourselves, and by choosing that path see a measure of growth and healing in our lives and the lives of others around us. But what prevents us from forgiving?

I personally feel that the choice is not *"Should* I forgive?" but *"How* do I forgive?" Many of us move into a place where we want to move forward in life and not stay in bitterness, making the same broken choices out of our wounding. It is at that point we need to ask ourselves *how* we can forgive ourselves and others.

I think one question should be: What *is* forgiveness? So many of us don't walk out forgiveness due to the simple fact that we ourselves have not been educated or shown a healthy example in our personal relationship of what forgiveness looks like.

Forgiveness is trusting God with what has been done to you as well as trusting God with what you have done with the situation. It means that we don't want to expose others for the sake of embarrassment. Forgiveness means that to the best of your ability you do whatever you can to ensure that all parties involved keep their dignity.

154

It sometimes seems like we want to tell as many people as possible about what someone has done to us. We don't want that person to get off scot-free with hurting us. This is where we must be careful when walking out our process of forgiveness. We often want to punish others or hurt them for what they have done. We can't stand the idea of someone not paying for what "they" have done to us.

One of the most difficult hurdles that we must cross when dealing with the issue of forgiveness is feeling like the issue is too much for us. We can feel like the circumstances and events that have landed us in this battle are just too painful and too big to allow forgiveness. But we must learn to take our pain to God and grow beyond bitterness in order to forgive both ourselves and others.

Questions

1. Are you hiding bitterness in your heart? What steps can you take to expose and destroy hidden bitterness?

2. Do you find it nearly impossible to forgive someone who deceived or lied to you? Do you continue to hold bitterness toward that person(s)?

3. Have you found a false strength or identity in bitterness? Have you taken that pain, anger, or hurt and turned it into a defense mechanism?

4. True faith and true Christianity come from the survival of tragedy. Do you have a personal example that confirms this statement?

JESUS AND FORGIVENESS

In the New Testament, Jesus speaks of the importance of Christians forgiving or showing mercy toward others:

> *Blessed are the merciful, for they will be shown mercy* (Matthew 5:7 NIV).

> *Therefore, if you are offering your gift at the altar and there remember that your brother has something against you, leave your gift there in front of the altar. First go and be reconciled to your brother; then come and offer your gift* (Matthew 5:23-24 NIV).

> *And when you stand praying, if you hold anything against anyone, forgive him, so that your Father in heaven may forgive you your sins* (Mark 11:25 NIV).

But I tell you who hear Me: Love your enemies, do good to those who hate you, bless those who curse you, pray for those who mistreat you. If someone strikes you on one cheek, turn to him the other also (Luke 6:27-29 NIV).

Be merciful, just as your Father is merciful (Luke 6:36 NIV).

Do not judge, and you will not be judged. Do not condemn, and you will not be condemned. Forgive, and you will be forgiven (Luke 6:37 NIV).

Then Peter came to Him and said, "Lord, how often shall my brother sin against me, and I forgive him? Up to seven times?" Jesus said to him, "I do not say to you, up to seven times, but up to seventy times seven" (Matthew 18:21-22 NKJV).

Jesus was doing something that was really radical for the times He lived in. Jesus was bringing forth a new truth that would turn the religious mindset of His day on its ear. Jesus had this outstanding message of the total forgiveness of sins. What a marvelous grace the Father extended through Jesus! This is the economy of God that the uncreated God of the universe would show such over-extending love to all of His creation through the power of forgiveness.

An interesting thing that you learn about Jesus as you read the Gospels is that He didn't extend grace in a manner that took away our moral responsibility. Instead Jesus extended grace that gives us the ability to have moral responsibility. We can get very confused about grace at times. We forget that forgiveness is walking out grace for ourselves as well as for others. True grace will never take advantage of the character or nature of God.

We learn in the beatitudes that Jesus actually called the standards higher than the religious community of His day. When Peter came to Jesus to ask how many times he should extend forgiveness to someone else, Jesus replied, *"seventy times seven."* Jesus answered this way because the teachers of the law in Jesus' day actually put a cap on forgiveness. But Jesus said, "Go beyond what is required of you." When a heart controlled by love is at the helm, it is not as hard to make choices based out of that same love.

Most charismatic denominations teach that a believer receives forgiveness more directly through a sincere expression of repentance to God, and that the believer completes this in the act of forgiving others. Some denominations generally place more emphasis on the need for private or informal repentance, and less emphasis on the need for formal or public repentance. This is supported by the direction to confess to God, since He is the only one who can forgive sins.

However, even Catholics and Orthodox Christians cite scriptural support for a mediated confession, a power Jesus conferred upon the apostles to act in His name. I don't know where they came from but you can take them out if needed? Since the Church's very existence is formed by God's forgiveness, it operates as a people of forgiveness, forgiven and forgiving, inextricably tied to peacemaking and justice. Philip D. Kenneson, associate professor of theology and philosophy at Milligan College, writes in his book *Life on the Vine*:

God's intent was not that this one divine act of forgiveness [in Jesus Christ] would itself magically transform the creation into God's intended paradise. Rather, this supreme act of forgiveness in Christ is the very large rock dropped into the middle of a pond. …If I refuse such forgiveness [for others] in the name of justice, is it possible that my view of justice falls short of God's view, where justice, shalom, wholeness, and salvation are not opposing goals, but different names for God's singular desire?[1]

Questions

1. Jesus extended grace that gives you the ability to have moral responsibility. Do you sometimes forget that forgiveness is walking out grace for yourself as well as for others?

2. Of the Scripture passages cited at the beginning of the chapter, which one best symbolizes your perspective about Jesus and forgiveness? Why?

3. Have you been presented with the challenge of forgiving someone "seventy times seven"? How hard or easy was it for you?

4. Some churches place more emphasis on private or informal repentance, and less on the need for formal or public repentance. What is your belief about this topic?

Endnote

1. Wikipedia contributors, "Forgiveness," Wikipedia, The Free Encyclopedia, http://en.wikipedia.org/w/index.php?title

=Forgiveness&oldid=339120871; New World Encyclopedia contributors, "Forgiveness," New World Encyclopedia, http://www .newworldencyclopedia.org/entry/Forgiveness?oldid=899956; Philip D. Kenneson, *Life on the Vine: Cultivating the Fruit of the Spirit in Christian Community* (InterVarsity Press: 1999).

MOVING ON IN FORGIVENESS

The questions asked throughout this book have been *What do we do with our pain?* and *Where do we take our pain?* We have learned that we take our pain to the cross. We must take all of our disappointments, failures, and rejection to Jesus and let Him take it all.

I actually had a vision once when I was in a worship service, and it went like this:

I saw Jesus standing at the altar of the Church. I saw a line form in front of Jesus, stretching as far as the eye could see. I then was brought right up to the side of Jesus. A man walked up to Jesus and handed Him a porno magazine. Jesus smiled at the man and said, "Thank you so much." I was appalled at this vision and said to myself, *No, don't give Jesus that magazine!*

Then I looked and saw a woman approach Jesus and she started pounding on His chest and yelling in His face, saying, "How could You do this to me! I hate You!" She yelled till she was red in the face and then collapsed. The whole time she was hitting Him, Jesus was smiling, and He just kept saying, "Thank you." I said, "Stop hitting Him! STOP IT!"

Then another man approached Jesus and punched Him as hard as he could in the face and called Jesus a faggot. He screamed at Jesus and said, "Why can't You be a man! You are such a letdown and such a failure!" This man was screaming at Jesus and then fell at Jesus' feet sobbing and weeping. The man was covering his face, and Jesus bent down and removed this man's hands from his face and said, "Thank you," and smiled at the man.

I was shown another person, and then another, and another approach Jesus and whisper terrible dark things in His ear. Jesus just kept smiling and saying thanks. Over and over again, Jesus took every blow, every inappropriate thing, and still He just smiled and said "Thank you."

I was really upset with all these people and what they were doing to Jesus. And then the Lord spoke to me and said, "I must take it all. I must take all of it. Every bit of darkness that is surrendered to Me, I must take it and turn it into beauty. I must take this so they can move on in forgiveness." These people were giving Jesus everything that had been done to them or said about them. They were taking their wounds, rejection, abuse, and lack of forgiveness and putting them into Jesus, and He was just taking it all in. "When people are in their darkest moment, I will take it," Jesus said. "I will take it all; I will take it all...."

164

Forgiveness is a daily process and not a single final act. In order to move on in forgiveness, you must dedicate yourself to the process. It is very easy to delude yourself into thinking that what happened wasn't as big of a deal as you're making it out to be. The truth is that we must acknowledge what has been done and come to terms with the full weight of it. We find ourselves saying things like, "I thought I already dealt with this issue," or "I thought I already forgave this person." The truth is that when we say the words, "I forgive you," it's not an automatic fix for all the damage that has been done. I do believe that as you progressively forgive and say the words over and over again, choosing to believe, you will start to see the bitterness and unforgiveness leave your thoughts and your soul.

Part of the problem is that we do not address what it looks like for us to move on in forgiveness. To move on in forgiveness is to let go and to trust God with what has been done. We are bent as a culture on retribution, and there is a place for God to walk that out, but not for us. We should not hold others or ourselves hostage through refusing to move forward in forgiveness. When we face moving on, we feel as if we are going to go on, and no one will know what this person has done to us. The truth is that we can never really force anyone to take the responsibility for wounding us (minus illegal acts, which can be punished by the state).

Perception is a very powerful thing for us as it relates to moving on in forgiveness. Oftentimes, when we hurt others or someone has hurt us, a major issue has been "perception" and not necessarily truth. This can become dangerous when we as people take on the identity of what we perceive, versus   165 standing in the truth. I have met people who were hurt due to poor choices, immaturity, sin, or other very human reasons, and yet they chose to *become* their brokenness or bitterness, and it prevented them from moving forward in forgiveness.

I myself went through a large-scale rejection and wounding a few years back. I had to progressively walk out my healing and the areas in which I was responsible. The temptation arose through pain to become the victim or to hold onto that identity, rather than to forgive and move on in my true identity. I was fortunate enough to walk through healing and come out the other side of a very heart-breaking ordeal.

The enemy will do what he can to keep you stuck in your history. Many times during this personal season of hardship, satan came and whispered very harmful things to me. The enemy said things like, "Where is your friend Jesus?" or "Maybe you're just not a good Christian." These were stupid statements to which I already knew the answer in my head, but it was my heart that was damaged. The enemy can change your perception of a situation very easily, especially when sin is in the mix.

I would like to say that the other people who have hurt me or whom I have hurt were able to rise above in truth and walk out their true identity, but that has not always been the case. Many people I have known, some old friends, some old romances, some old business partners, have overcome the wounds of broken situations and moved on in forgiveness, and yet some have chosen to stay in a false truth about who they are or who God is. Moving forward is the only progression left for those wanting a future. We never truly solve a problem like this; we simply go through it and get the option to become stronger and wiser, or we stay in our brokenness, alone, isolated, and immature.

We must not become too hung up on the idea of closure, as we know it. I have counseled several people who feel that if they can just get that final honest answer from the source who wounded them, they can move on. Often that is a desperate idea that the enemy will use to keep you stuck in your pain. You cannot look to the source of your wounding to find your healing. So much of moving on does come with closure, but you do not need to necessarily receive closure from that individual. You can get closure from coming to terms with what has taken place.

You cannot allow your history to keep you bound up in the past. You must choose to move forward and walk it out. You can tell your story to an accountability partner or a counselor without it becoming gossip or an attempt to shame someone else.

Communication is such a helpful aspect of the healing and forgiving process. When we are able to talk out our feelings and emotions, versus acting them out, we find ourselves in a much healthier and less damaging process of healing. As a culture, we have become very comfortable acting out or reacting instead of talking out our emotions. We tend to keep things bottled up inside of us until the moment we boil over, and at that point we lose our cool and pop our top, so to speak.

To move on in forgiveness means to feel the full spectrum of emotion in your situation. I am not talking about letting the enemy breathe on your circumstances, but about allowing God to breathe upon your emotions. It is OK to feel angry. It is OK to feel hurt or sad, but it is when those things control us that we walk in an unredeemed emotional state. Emotions like resentment and unresolved hurt come to the surface and cloud our willingness or ability to move past our wounds. God created you uniquely, which means that your journey through pain and hurt will be equally unique to a degree. We are to embrace the healing process, not prolong it.

Myths About Forgiveness

Through a lack of education and experience, we as a culture deal with many myths about forgiveness. Some of the myths we deal with are as follows:

1. If I forgive, then I approve what was done to me.

2. If I forgive, my relationship with the person I am forgiving will improve and return to normal.

3. If I forgive the individual, I will automatically be free from anger or resentment toward them.

4. If I remember and acknowledge what was done to me, then I haven't forgotten and thus I haven't fully forgiven.

5. It is not important to forgive myself in the process of forgiving others.

I know it may sound totally "spiritual" to say that you must pray for those whom you need to forgive, but that is the spiritual truth. In order to get the healing and closure we need, we must pray for those whom we have hurt and who have hurt us. This is a model that Jesus walked out in His life; and when it counted most (on the cross), He chose to petition the Father on the behalf of those who were nailing Him to a tree. Everything Jesus walked out in His human form He made accessible to us as His children. When Jesus chose to forgive someone, He made it possible for us to walk in that same forgiveness, as well as giving us the same power through the Holy Spirit to forgive with the same strength that He forgave.

When we pray for someone we need to forgive, we must pray from a positive heart posture. This means that we must pray with the right motives. I have had people ask me if it is OK to pray for someone to be in pain or have a miserable life because of what they did to them. This is a shocking question to me because the answer is obvious…NO. When you pray for someone and your motives are twisted concerning that individual, then it's called "witchcraft."

To pray for someone means to pray for God's best for them and their lives. That is always the answer when lifting someone up in prayer. This means that you pray for that person who has hurt you to have success, wisdom, beauty, and general good things. We pray for people to have a spirit of wisdom and revelation. To forgive someone is to pray for them to prosper.

Questions

1. What does forgiveness look like for you?

2. Can you pray for the healing, freedom, and success of the person whom you have hurt or who has hurt you?

3. Can you tell your story of abuse, shame, or rejection without giving away the identity of the one who has hurt you? Can you pray for God to not hold them accountable for what they've done?

4. Can you forgive yourself for missing the mark or hurting others?

5. Did Jesus show us the importance of forgiveness?

6. Do an exercise: Write down all the examples you can find in the Word on forgiveness, and then contemplate on those examples.

Conclusion

As we wrestle with our ideas of community along with the great gift we have been entrusted with, let us create a culture that is grounded in identity, love, and truth. It is a very hard thing to be a Christian and to live in a community of believers, but what I am hoping and praying is that this book was able to be a source of strength to persevere.

The process of writing this book has been really wonderful and difficult. I have relived situations that were incredibly hard and painful as well as incredibly beautiful. I am praying that you have also found yourself going through the same journey. I pray that as you have been brave and faced your pain, you have discovered a place where you could start the journey of finding yourself again.

In doing the research for this book, I found that the way we think about how God feels about us greatly determines our view of the future as well as our level of success in our current situations. We must trust that we are loved by God and that He has a great future planned for us full of love, success, beauty, and growth. We can face our "NOW" moments when we believe that we have a future of hope and that God is interested in us. If we can live out of the reality of our future, beautiful life, then we can live in that place in the NOW! We can trust the Lord with our future, and by doing that, we can trust Him now with our lives. We must believe in who Jesus says we are to progressively move forward. The absence of commitment to the future brings an identity crisis in the present.

We need to be reminded of who we are in the midst of our pain. We must be dedicated to our spiritual well-being as well as our identity. I can't tell you how many people I've spoken with during the course of writing this book who have lost themselves in the grind of life. I am aware now more than ever of the importance of letting the Holy Spirit give us the ability to keep our individuality and uniqueness. I am hoping that this book was able to be a beacon of hope as it relates to defrosting from pain, rejection, and spiritual abuse.

What are your future goals for moving forward in your identity? Many people have no concrete goals. It will do us good to extend the effort to picture, if you can, what your future holds. You have a hope and a truth to align yourself with, so that you are not doomed to be a rejected Christian.

To those of you who have been spiritually abused and involved with church splits: you must realize that you are not destined to be an outsider, and that it is OK to trust God in your situations. For all of you who are hiding from church due to pain, I am hoping this book calls you out of hiding and that you are able to return and help produce a counter-culture that helps the Church become a safe place again.

I want to encourage all who read this book to reach for the stars. So many of us through abuse learn that when we reach for the stars, we get smacked out of the sky. Well, now you know that you can put off your fear of man and reach as high as you can for God with no fear of rejection or of getting your wings clipped. You are free to make a game plan of your future success. You don't need to be consumed by the worry that the other shoe will drop. You can be committed to and believe in *"Christ in you, the hope of Glory"* (Col. 1:27)!